MIGHTY
MUSCLE
CARS

BY THE AUTO EDITORS OF CONSUMER GUIDE®

Publications International, Ltd.

Louis Weber, CEO
Publications International, Ltd.
7373 North Cicero Avenue
Lincolnwood, Illinois 60712

Manufactured in China.

8 7 6 5 4 3 2 1

ISBN-13: 978-1-4127-1203-3
ISBN-10: 1-4127-1203-3

Library of Congress Control Number: 2005922659

Thanks to the following for their contributed materials:
DaimlerChrysler AG; Ford Motor Company; General Motors Photographic Archive; The Harry Kapsalis Collection; National Hot Rod Association; Frank Peiler.

Thanks to the following photographers:
Roger Barnes; Ken Beebe; Joe Bohovic; Chan Bush; Mark Garcia; Thomas Glatch; Jerry Heasley; Don Heiny; Vince Manocchi; Doug Mitchel; Mike Mueller; David Newhardt; Frank Peiler; Rasputin Studios; Jeff Rose; Tom Roster; Tom Shaw; Mike Spenner; Richard Spiegelman; Tom Storm; David Temple; Phil Toy; Rob Van Schaick; W.C. Waymack; Nicky Wright.

Thanks to the owners of the cars featured in this book:
Bob Anderson; Norman Andrews; Dennis A. Barnes; Larry Bell; Rich Bruhn; Rodney Brumbaugh; Jerry & Carol Buczkowski; Patt & J.R. Buxman; Rick Cain; Greg and Cecilia Carter; June Cecil; Classic Car Centre, Inc.; Jerry Coffee; Glenn Cole; Dr. Randy and Freda Cooper; Robert Costa; "Basketball Sam" Davis; Terry D. Davis; Craig J. Dawson; Harry DeMenge; Tim Dusek; Ray & Gil Elias; James & Mary Engle; Phil Fair; Robert Fraser; Gil Garcia; Allan Gartzman; Alden Graber; Michael S. Gray; Denny Guest; Michael Hakkert; Henry Hart; Michael E. Hatch; Bill Hoff; Jimmy Hollywood; Cherie Jacobson; Chris & Greg Joseph; Robert & Ann Klein; Jim Labertew; Richard P. Lambert; Guy Mabee; Bob Macy; Larry G. Maisel; Browney L. Mascow; Bob Mason; Harry J. & Carol S. Miller; Larry & Karen Miller; Mr. & Mrs. Richard D. Miller; Ralph Milner; Earl Morgan; Bob Mosher; Ronald S. Mroz; Yoshio & Eric Nakayama; Barbara Nave; Terry Nelson; Rich Neubauer; Sam Pierce; Glenn Quealy; Bruce Rambler; Alan Ranz; Jim Regnier; Joseph H. Risner; Keith Rohm; Jim & John Russell; Steve Schappaugh; Gary Schneider; Show N Tell Muscle Car Classics; Candy & Tom Spiel; Frank Spittle; Nathan Struder; Tom & Nancy Stump; Brian Thomason; Dick Towers; Jerry Trelevan; Bob Trevarrow; Barry Troup; Nick Van DeWater; Mike Venarde; Volo Auto Museum; Randy & Jean Williams; Sam Williford; Patrick Wnek; George Young; Michael Zawozski; Chris Zinn.

Contents

Foreword

Muscle cars had stripes. But not all cars with stripes were muscle cars. Muscle cars had scoops. But not all cars with scoops were muscle cars. Muscle cars had bucket seats. But...

You get the idea.

Mighty Muscle Cars celebrates a singular breed of American performance machine at its early-1960s to early-'70s zenith. By strict definition, a muscle car was a midsize two-door model with a large V-8 engine, though the term also embraced certain full-size models, a few compacts, and some ponycars.

To even pretend to the title, however, a car's focus had to be mad acceleration. Sometimes the finish line was a drag-strip timing beam. Sometimes it was the next stoplight.

As for that business about stripes, scoops, and bucket seats: *Mighty Muscle Cars* certainly includes the hot rides that dressed flashy. And it loves them in racing livery. But it flat ignores the pretenders that had the look but couldn't cook.

Its heart might be said to lie with the big-block predators that had no taste for stripes, no use for pretend scoops. Our consummate muscle cars are snarling wallflowers with vinyl bench seats and factory lightweights with wrinkle-wall slicks. Got a problem with that?

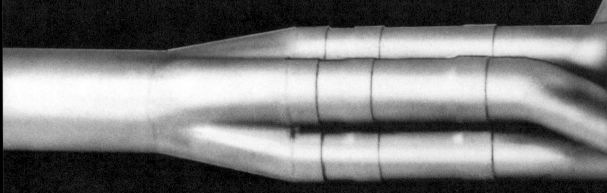

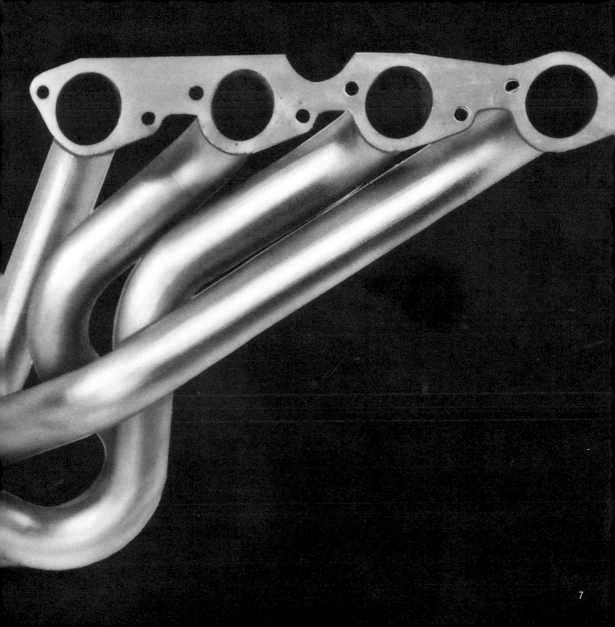

After spending the majority of the Sixties resisting the trend toward high-performance cars, American Motors finally jumped on the muscle car bandwagon with the 1968 Javelin and AMX. The Javelin was a four-seat pony-car; the AMX was a short-wheelbase, two-seat "sports car" variant. Most AMX buyers stepped up to the top engine option, a 315-hp 390. Underneath was a heavy-duty suspension, a beefy front sway bar, and a pair of trailing arms that acted like traction bars to fight rear-axle hop. A "Go" package added power front disc brakes, E70x14 tires, Twin-Grip limited slip, and racing stripes.

Factory-backed Javelin race cars debuted in the 1968 SCCA Trans Am season. Below, AMC team drivers John Martin and Don White pose in their 1969 Javelins in a staged publicity photo. AMC made a good showing, but trailed Chevrolet and Ford in Trans Am points standings in both '68 and '69. Javelins showed up at the dragstrips as well—this dealer-sponsored Javelin ran mid- to low-11's in Super Stock/Automatic. Street Javelins received mild facelifts and revised striping for 1969.

RACY.

In 1969, AMC teamed with Hurst to add some muscle to its staid Rambler Rogue compact. The car debuted midway through the model year as the AMC SC/Rambler Hurst; most called it the Scrambler. Under the scooped hood was a 315-hp 390 hooked to a four speed. All SC/Ramblers wore one of two red, white, and blue paint schemes.

A 1969 AMX bites hard off the line at the 1970 NHRA Winternationals. Note the wrinkling slicks; drag racers ran very low air pressure in their rear tires to enhance traction. Like their Javelin siblings, AMXs were little changed for the 1969 season. A couple of welcome updates were a 140-mph speedometer and the replacement of AMC's balky shift linkage with a Hurst setup.

Who's afraid of the Big Bad Colors?

Big Bad Javelin

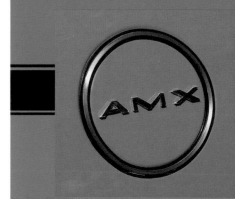

Optional Big Bad Orange,
Big Bad Blue or Big Bad Green
paint—includes painted front
and rear bumpers.

Optional Adjust-O-Tilt steering
wheel.

Optional Twin-Grip differential.

Optional "Go" Package.
(Includes 343 or 390 V-8, dual
exhausts, power disc brakes,
E70 X 14 Red Line tires,
handling package and black
fiberglass hood scoops.)

Optional dual exhausts.
(Standard with 390 engine.)

Optional roof spoiler.

Optional 140 mph speedometer
and big faced tach.

Optional "C" rally stripe.

Optional exhaust-style trim
panels.

Optional E70 X 14 Goodyear
Polyglas™ Red Line tires.

Optional AMX 390 cu. in.
engine. (High-performance
dealer installed AM parts
plus "Isky," Edelbrock,
Offenhauser and Doug's Headers
parts available for this engine,
if you want to modify it.)

Optional power disc brakes.

Optional mag-style wheels.

Optional air-conditioning.

Optional 4-speed close-ratio gear
box with Hurst shifter.

Optional Airless Spare.

Optional 8-track stereo tape
with AM radio.

Optional handling package.
(Includes heavy-duty
springs and shocks plus beefed
up anti-sway bar.)

American Motors

Vibrant "mod" paint hues were a muscle car trend; AMC's "Big Bad Colors" were a mid-1969 addition to AMC's lineup. For just $34 extra, buyers could have their 1969 Javelin or AMX decked out in Big Bad Orange, Big Bad Green, or Big Bad Blue. Color-keyed bumpers were also part of the package.

Hip name, loud stripes, white-letter tires, bulging hood scoop, raked stance... AMC employed every hot-car dress-up trick in the book for the 1970 Rebel Machine. The ad department even whipped up promotional stickers with a far-out cartoon hippie. All Machines got a 340-hp, 390-cid four-barrel and a ram air system that employed a vacuum-controlled hood scoop. A tachometer was integrated into a raised fairing on the scoop in front of the driver. The first 1000 or so came in a wild red, white, and blue color scheme, but later the cars were offered in any 1970 AMC color.

For 1970, Javelins were facelifted again with a "twin-venturi" grille and optional twin-scooped ram-air hood. The "Big Bad" colors were still available, and AMC even built a few production Javelins in a Matador Red/Frost White/Commodore Blue combo to match its Trans Am race cars. AMC lured team owner Roger Penske and his star driver Mark Donohue over from Chevrolet for the 1970 Trans Am season. The special edition Mark Donohue Javelin wore an exclusive rear spoiler.

Donohue puts his mark on the Javelin.

Like the Javelin, the AMX was mildly freshened for 1970. A $384 "Go" package added E70x14 tires, front disc brakes, super heavy-duty suspension, limited slip diff, ram air, and improved engine cooling. The AMX would be demoted to a decor option for the redesigned Javelin for the '71 model year.

A FINE QUALITY-INDY INSPIRED

RACING JACKET

at a fraction of the usual cost!

We can't mention the name of the manufacturer but it's a leader in the racing apparel field...a famous name brand you'll recognize immediately!

HERE'S THE DEAL!
A FAMOUS MAKE RACING JACKET *PLUS* 24 BIG ISSUES OF HOT ROD ALL FOR ONLY $15.00

100% 2-ply OXFORD NYLON ● GUARANTEED COLOR FAST ● CERTIFIED WATER REPELLENT...NORANE TREATED ● RUST & SNAG PROOF ZIPPER ● COMFORTABLE ELASTIC CUFFS ● ACCESSORY POCKETS ● OFFICIAL CAR EMBLEM ...EMBROIDERED—COLOR FAST ● MATCHING RACING STRIPES

TO: HOT ROD 5900 Hollywood Blvd., Los Angeles, Calif. 90028   HRH33

Send me my famous make Racing Jacket with the emblem and size indicated below...and also the next 24 issues of HOT ROD MAGAZINE.
My check or money order for $15.00* is enclosed.

EMBLEM	JACKET COLOR	TRIM	S	M	L	XL
☐ CAMARO	STEEL BLUE	WHITE/RED	☐	☐	☐	☐
☐ CHEVROLET	NAVY BLUE	WHITE/RED	☐	☐	☐	☐
☐ CORVETTE	NAVY BLUE	GOLD/RED	☐	☐	☐	☐
☐ COUGAR	NAVY BLUE	WHITE	☐	☐	☐	☐
☐ DODGE	RED	WHITE	☐	☐	☐	☐
☐ FORD	WHITE	BLUE/RED	☐	☐	☐	☐
☐ GTO	RED	WHITE/BLACK	☐	☐	☐	☐
☐ MUSTANG	WHITE	BLUE/RED	☐	☐	☐	☐
☐ PLYMOUTH	LT. BLUE	WHITE	☐	☐	☐	☐
☐ FIREBIRD	RED	WHITE/BLACK	☐	☐	☐	☐
☐ OLDS 442	GOLD	BLACK/WHITE	☐	☐	☐	☐

NAME _____

ADDRESS _____

CITY _____

STATE _____ ZIP _____

*Canada and other countries add $2.00 for postage.

ORDER YOUR RACING JACKET TODAY...SAVE! SAVE! SAVE!

25

Buick stepped into the muscle car fray with the 1965 Skylark Gran Sport. Advertising called it "A Howitzer With Windshield Wipers." The Gran Sport option package cost $250 more than a regular Skylark, and added a 401-cid V-8 that made 325 hp in stock form, 338 with dealer-installed dual quads. Buick called this engine a 400 so it would slip past the GM corporate edict that limited engines in midsized cars to 400 cubic inches.

All of GM's intermediates were handsomely restyled for 1966, the Skylark included. Gran Sports were distinguished externally by emblems, a blacked-out grille, and faux hood scoops/front-fender vents. The base 401-cid "Wildcat 445" four barrel had 325 hp, but a hotter 340-hp version was made available during the model year. The 340-hp engine redlined at 4600 rpm and made a peak 445 lb/ft of torque at 3200. Gran Sports weren't the fastest big-cube intermediates, but they were among the best balanced.

Get in with the in Crowd in a GS

IN
'67 BUICK

The Skylark was mildly facelifted for '67, and Buick added a "junior super car" model, the GS 340 (below). Available in only white or silver, both with red accents, the GS 340 packed a 260-hp 340. Meanwhile, the GS 400 lost its "nailhead" 401 and gained a more modern 400-cid V-8 (right). The 400 was good for 340 hp and quarter-mile times in the high 14-second range.

For 1968, the GS 350 (below) replaced the GS 340 as junior partner to the GS 400 (right). The GS 350 had a 280-hp 350, while the GS 400 once again packed a 340-hp 400. The '69 GSs (far right) got revised trim and functional hood scoops. With their swoopy bodyside character creases and semiskirted rear wheel openings, these Skylarks didn't look like manly street brawlers. GS 400 versions had plenty of muscle though, especially with the optional Stage 1 package.

Light your fire.

BUICK MOTOR DIVISION

Warm up to one of the light-your-fire Buicks, the 1970 Buick GS 455 Stage I.

What is Stage I? It begins with a modified version of Buick's new 455 cubic-inch V8. It gets you a high-lift cam, a big Quadrajet carburetor, a low-restriction dual exhaust system, heavy-duty valve springs and cooling system, even functional hood scoops. It delivers 360 horsepower, 510 foot/pounds of torque.

After more? You can order an extra heavy-duty Rallye suspension with front and rear track bars. You can add G60x15 super wide ovals, front disc brakes and replace the standard three-speed manual transmission with a specially-calibrated Turbo-Hydramatic or floor-mounted, Hurst-linked four-speed manual.

The 1970 Buick GS 455 Stage I. It's the enthusiast's machine you've been asking us to build.

Consider it built.

Now, wouldn't you really rather have a Buick.

STAGE 1

GSs got a brawnier look for 1970. A bargain at $199, the Stage 1 package added heaps of hi-po goodies, including a 3.64:1 Positraction rear axle and performance mods to the available three- and four-speed manuals and the automatic.

The Stage 1 455 was very conservatively rated by the factory at 360 hp, but its torque output—a stump-pulling 510 lb/ft at a mere 2800 rpm—showed its true strength. This prodigious low-end grunt made a Stage 1 Buick a feared competitor on the street or the strip. A properly equipped Stage 1 was more than capable of running with a Hemi.

GSX

Buick's GSX.
A limited edition.

Another light-your-fire car
from Buick.

The GSX package added an upgraded suspension, hood tach, stripes, spoilers, and $1195 to a 1970 GS 455. Saturn Yellow or Apollo White were the only available colors. The 1971 GSXs (below left) came in a choice of six colors, but power was down to 345 hp in top-line Stage 1 form. All '71 GS engines were detuned to run on low-lead fuel.

The Stage 1 package was ordered on only 801 GS coupes for 1971, a sign of the muscle car's waning popularity with the new-car-buying public. *Motor Trend*'s 1971 Stage 1 did the quarter in 14.7 seconds at 92.5 mph. A sliding fabric sunroof was a novel option for 1972, but the Stage 1 455 was now down to 270 net horsepower.

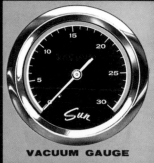

The formation of the NHRA's Super
Stock classes in the mid-Fifties helped
fan the flames of Detroit's "horsepower race." Chevrolet followed up its
revolutionary 1955 small-block V-8s
with the 348-cid "W-motor" in 1958.
Here, a pair of 348-powered 1960
Chevys square off at the '62 NHRA
Winternationals. For '61, Chevrolet
dealt a one-two punch with the introduction of Super Sport package and
the soon-to-be-famous 409.

IT FEELS GOOD, LOOKS BETTER and GOES GREAT!

Take any one of Chevy's five '61 Impalas, add either the new 409-cubic-inch V8 or the 348-cubic-inch job and a four-speed floor-mounted stick, wrap the whole thing in special trim that sets it apart from any other car on the street, and man, you have an Impala Super Sport! Every detail of this new Chevrolet package is custom made for young men on the move. This is the kind of car the insiders mean when they say _Chevy_, the kind that can only be appreciated by a man who understands, wants, and won't settle for less than REAL driving excitement.

Here are the ingredients of the Impala Super Sport kit* • Special Super Sport trim, inside and out • Instrument Panel Pad • Special wheel covers • Power brakes and power steering • Choice of five power teams: 305 hp. with 4-speed Synchro-Mesh or heavy-duty Powerglide, 348 hp. with 4-speed only, 250 hp. with 4-speed only, 380 hp. with 4-speed only • Heavy-duty springs and shocks • Sintered metallic brake linings • 7,000-RPM Tach • 8.00 x 14 narrow band whitewalls • Chevrolet Division of General Motors, Detroit 2, Michigan.

*Optional at extra cost, as a complete kit only.

Lighter in weight and $100 cheaper than an Impala, Chevrolet's Bel Air sport coupe was a popular choice among 409 buyers in 1962. The base single-quad 409 had 380 hp. With twin Carter AFB four barrels and a wild cam, the 409 developed a rated 409 horsepower at 6000 rpm, and 420 lb/ft of torque at 4000, on 11.0:1 compression. Dig the fenderwell headers and super-long traction bars on Jerry Latschap's "Super Duck" Bel Air.

Chevy 409 V8 — JOB

REMARKS — *Son of a gun!*

BORE
4.3125

STROKE
3.50

GROSS HORSEPOWER
409 @ 6000

GROSS TORQUE (LB. FT.)
420 @ 4000

COMPRESSION RATIO
11 to 1

DISPLACEMENT (CU. IN.)
409

CHEVROLET

Amazing! This engine, available as an extra-cost option, turns a perfectly normal Chevrolet into something else altogether. It's available as shown with two aluminum four-barrels and a special cam or in a slightly tamer version with one four-barrel and a mere 380 horsepower. If performance is your meat, this engine'll give you just about all the protein a feller could use. Check the chart!

CHEVROLET DIVISION OF GENERAL MOTORS, DETROIT 2, MICHIGAN

DYNO-TUNED by DON NICHOLSON   SERV

At the 1962 NHRA Winternationals, "Dyno Don" Nicholson won the Stock Eliminator title for the second straight year behind the wheel of a super-tuned 409.

The Chevy II compact bowed for 1962, with four- and six-cylinder power. Hot rodders were soon shoehorning in V-8s. Dick Rutherford ran this one with a fuel-injected 327 Corvette engine at the 1962 NHRA Winternationals. Below, 18-year-old Butch Leal wheels a Stock Eliminator Impala at the '63 Winternationals. The Super Stock drag cars of this era adopted a nose-high stance as racers attempted to achieve better weight transfer and traction off the line.

The "civilian" 1963 Chevrolet engine roster topped out at a 425-hp 409, but a select few factory-approved buyers could get a limited-production 427-cid version of the 409 called the Z-11. This exotic dual-quad mill made 430 hp at 6000 rpm, 425 lb/ft of torque at 4200. Z-11s used a special air cleaner/plenum that ducted fresh air in from the cowl vent. The sprung hood and open headlight buckets on the Impala at lower right were other early methods of cold air induction.

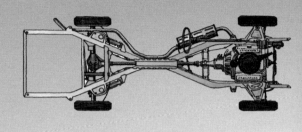

Chevy's 409 was carried over into 1964 with no major changes. As before, Impala SS hardtops had the most glitz, but the sleeper car of choice was the low-budget Biscayne two-door sedan. Meadow Green paint, sparse chrome, taxicab hubcaps, and a bench seat are good for stealth. A 425-hp 409, M20 four speed, and 3.70:1 Positraction rear end are good for smoke.

Chevrolet's Chevelle debuted in 1964. Though it didn't yet pack big-block power, the new bowtie intermediate could be a peppy performer in topline Malibu SS trim. Initially, a 220-hp 283 was the top engine, but the success of Pontiac's GTO compelled Chevrolet to pick up the pace. Hence, the 327-cid small-block V-8 was added to the arsenal in mid-1964, in 250- or 300-hp tune.

Chevrolet's full-size cars gained a more voluptuous "Coke bottle" shape for 1965. The Impala SS started out the season with a 340- or 400-hp 409 as its top engine choice. At midyear, the 409 was replaced by the all-new 396-cid Mark IV big-block V-8—the first of Chevrolet's popular "rat" motors. The inaugural 396 put out 425 horsepower in top tune.

The 1965 Malibu SS (above right) was available over the counter with spunky 327-cid small blocks, but they couldn't hang with the competition's big-cube brawlers. Chevrolet rectified the situation in mid-1965 with the limited-edition Malibu SS Z-16. A mere 201 were produced, all with special trim, heavy-duty suspension, and a potent 375-hp, 396-cid big block.

TURBO-JET 427 V8

do not tease

Chevy rebored its 396 V-8 in mid-1966, expanding it to 427 cubic inches. In street tune, the Mark IV big block had 390 hp; a "special performance" solid-lifter version with a four-bolt main block gave 425. Still, full-size stormers were quickly being eclipsed on the street and on the track by hot intermediates and compacts, including the smartly restyled Chevy II Nova. Though the compact Nova couldn't carry a big-cube motor without serious modifications, the hot small-block-powered cars were plenty potent. Bill "Grumpy" Jenkins turned ETs in the high 11s with his L79 327-powered Chevy II Novas (above and overleaf).

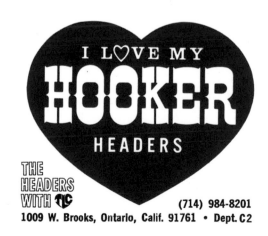

The SS 396 was the new top-of-the-line Chevelle series for 1966. Obviously, all got a 396. The 325-hp Turbo Jet was standard, but a 360-hp L34 version or the solid-lifter 375-hp L78 were optional. SS 396s came only as two-door hardtops or convertibles. The red convertible is a one-off GM show car with a unique power-bulge hood and five-spoke mag wheels. Most production SS 396s left the factory with faux mag-look wheelcovers and redline tires, as shown on this Tuxedo Black hardtop.

It took Chevrolet a couple of years to field a competitor to Ford's Mustang, but the new-for-'67 Camaro hit the ponycar target squarely. SS versions got stiffer springs and shocks, F70x14 Firestone Wide Oval tires, performance hood, and "bumblebee" nose stripes. A 295-hp 350 was available from the start, but a 375-hp 396 was added later in the year. A $105 Rally Sport option package added a hidden-head-lamp grille and other appearance tweaks.

Headers up, Camaro! You're in Cyclone Country!

A new nation has emerged. We call it Cyclone Country, because it's any place where you see, use or buy Cyclone Hi-Performance Products, like our Chevy 4-tube Competi-tion Headers. Each set has been precision-formed on the most modern machines in the world. And each set has been spe-cially engineered to give you maximum horse-power from that tiger you drive. Raw. Gutsy. That's what Cyclone products mean to you. And if that's what you want, move into Cyclone Country. You'll never leave.

Shown: Cyclone's Chevrolet 4-Tube Competition Headers.

CYCLONE
AUTOMOTIVE PRODUCTS
3402 Winona Ave./Burbank, Calif. 91503

The World's largest producer of high performance Headers, Mufflers, Dual Exhaust Systems, Custom Exhaust Components, Safety Roll Bars and Portable Engine Stands. Watch for your Cyclone Country Club Membership Card. It comes with every Cyclone exhaust system....It's valuable!

Command Performance

The 1967 SS 396 Chevelles sported a crisp facelift and some new options. The power bulge hood vents looked great, but weren't functional. Super Sports cost about $285 more than comparable Malibu models. Ordering the $121 power front-disc brake option brought Rally-style 14-inch slotted wheels to replace the usual small hubcaps or SS wheel-covers. The 375-hp L78 396 was no longer listed in sales brochures, but did remain a $476 dealer-installed conversion fitted into 612 cars.

Midsized cars were the most popular platforms for muscle cars, but many manufacturers still offered compact and full-size performance-car packages. The Chevy Nova SS could again be ordered with the potent L79 327 engine, basically a Corvette motor. With this engine, it could run with many larger big-block cars. Impalas could be had in SS 427 guise with special trim, stiffer springs and shocks, and a front stabilizer bar. For those who preferred more anonymity, the 427 was also available in plain-Jane Impalas.

Chevy II much.

Topside, it's a neat little two-door. Underneath, it's all set to move. Beefed-up suspension, wide oval red stripes and one of the greatest V8s you've ever ordered into action. It's a 350-cu.-in. 295-hp affair with 4-barrel carburetion and 2¼″ dual exhausts. Nova SS. We call it Chevy II much. You'll second the motion.

Chevy II Novas were redesigned for 1968, and lost the "Chevy II" monicker in 1969. A 295-hp 350 was initially the top engine choice, but big-block power was soon available. Bill "Grumpy" Jenkins continued his winning ways on the dragstrips with new Camaros and Novas. Jenkins' sponsors were quick to play up their racing credibility in advertising.

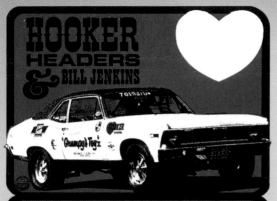

The Malibu/Chevelle was handsomely redesigned for 1968. The base 396 again had 325 hp, but another $237 netted the 375-hp L78. The top-dog L78 had solid lifters, big-port heads, and an 800-cfm Holley four barrel on a low-rise aluminum manifold. The factory four speed linkage was often difficult to shift quickly, prompting many owners to upgrade their machines with aftermarket Hurst shifters.

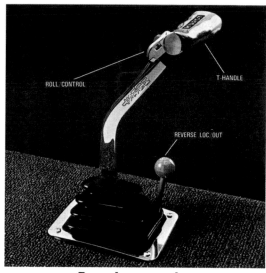

ROLL/CONTROL

T-HANDLE

REVERSE LOC OUT

For winners only.

If winning means more to you than eating or sleeping, we'll give you some friendly advice.

First, you've got to have a Hurst shifter. If you haven't, you're a natural born loser to begin with. Once you've got a Hurst you're practically there. Still, if you're really sincere about winning, you're not going to leave anything to chance. You'll add the key Hurst shifter accessories that give you that extra advantage and single you out as a guy who knows what it's all about.

Consistent-shift T-handle. Finger-contoured design assures exact hand placement for consistently perfect shifts. Handle is machine-angled to correspond exactly to the shifter's acceleration ramps.

Brake-holding Roll/Control. An electrically operated control that hooks into the brake system front and/or rear. Come to a stop, press the switch and take your foot off the brake pedal. Use it as a hill holder. Or as a guarantee against ever getting beat at the starting line again.

Reverse Loc/Out. A mechanical positive loc/out that backs up our patented 4-speed reverse inhibitor system for all-out competition. For normal use, when you may be backing up frequently, the standard 4-speed spring inhibitor is all the protection you need.

These are the items that spell the difference between winners and losers. You don't have to take our word for it. Ask any of the pro drivers who use them—any of the big names who drive for a living and depend on consistent winning to bring home the bucks. Then tell us if you'd like literature on any of the products described here. Hurst Performance Products, Warminster, Pennsylvania 18974.

HURST

GET ONE,
BEFORE ONE GETS YOU!

PHASE III

SS-427 CAMARO-$3795.00

STANDARD EQUIPMENT: 425 hp 427 engine, close-ratio Muncie four-speed; any ratio Posi rear; HD suspension and radiator; Wide Ovals; chrome valve covers; distinctive emblems & striping; bucket seats; modified ignition & dyno tune.

* SEND .50¢ for your copy of our '69½ Fantastic Five Chevrolet supercar & speed equipment racer's net catalog *

THE BALDWIN-MOTION PERFORMANCE COMBINE: BALDWIN CHEVROLET/Merrick Road & Central Avenue/Baldwin, L.I., N.Y./516-223-7700 MOTION PERFORMANCE, INC./High-Performance Sales-Service Division/599 Sunrise Highway/Baldwin, L.I., N.Y./516-223-3172-3178

Outrageous!

Let's face it troops, what else could you call a PHASE III supercar that comes stock with 427 cubes, 500 hp, three-barrel carb, tuned tube headers, M/P-Mallory Capacitive Discharge ignition, Schiefer-Lakewood goodies, Super-Bite suspension, scooped hood, ad infinitum. (There are even PHASE III 396-cube models available.) Not to mention that it's quicker and faster than anything Detroit has to offer. Last year it was Something Else. This year it's Outrageous. Next year? Personally, we're afraid to think that far ahead!

SS-427 CHEVELLE

SS-427 NOVA   SS-427 CAMARO

SS-427 CORVETTE

Send $1.00 for our all-new '69½ 396/427 Super-Chevy catalog

THE BALDWIN-MOTION PERFORMANCE GROUP BALDWIN CHEVROLET/Merrick Road & Central Avenue/Baldwin, L.I., 516-223-7700 MOTION PERFORMANCE, INC./High-Performance Sales-Service Division/599 Sunrise Highway/Baldwin, L.I., N.Y./516-223-3172-3178

WANTED
◆ PHASE III CAMARO ◆
By everyone who understands what torque, horsepower and really super cars are all about!

DESCRIPTION
Weight — 3,300 lbs. • Horsepower — 500 • Torque — unreal • Displacement — 427 cubes • Performance — out of sight

IDENTIFYING MARKS
Functionally scooped 'glass hood • Status emblems • Authoritative rumble

Approach with caution, as the PHASE III Camaro is known to be loaded for bear and to have an outrageous attitude. One was last seen in the vicinity of

THE BALDWIN-MOTION PERFORMANCE GROUP BALDWIN CHEVROLET/Merrick Road & Central Avenue/Baldwin, L.I., 516-223-7700 MOTION PERFORMANCE, INC./High-Performance Sales-Service Division/599 Sunrise Highway/Baldwin, L.I., N.Y./516-223-3172-3178

bending minds and turning heads. We advise getting one before one gets you!

* Send $1.00 for our all-new giant 1969½ catalog *

At the height of the muscle car craze, many new-car dealerships doubled as speed shops, and a few even produced their own special-edition cars. Three of the most famous high-performance dealers were Baldwin Chevrolet in Baldwin, NY (home of Joel Rosen's Motion Performance cars), Yenko Chevrolet in Canonsburg, PA, and Nickey Chevrolet in Chicago, IL. Each offered specially built Chevys that performed above and beyond the factory offerings.

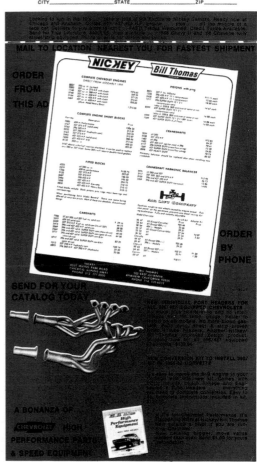

CHEVROLET SPORTS DEPARTMENT

84

The Chevelle SS 396 became a $348 Malibu option for 1969, but that didn't dim sales, which hit a record 86,307. The 375-hp L78 396 was again the top engine option. An estimated 400 buyers shelled out an additional $395 for the L89 option, which fit the L78 with weight-saving aluminum heads. If all that wasn't enough, buyers who were well-connected or especially savvy could snag a 425-hp 427-powered Chevelle via the Central Office Production Order (COPO) system. The COPO ordering process was intended for special-equipment fleet vehicles, but a few "with-it" managers bent the rules to slip through a few extra-potent muscle cars that weren't part of Chevy's normal model lineup.

The Hugger, Camaro SS Coupe with Rally Sport equipment.

What the younger generation's coming to.

The 1969 Camaro is closing the generation gap. Fast.

Some parents are even asking to borrow their kids' Camaros.

And some kids are actually letting them.

Camaro's secret is its Corvette accent. Standard bucket seats. V8's up to 325 horsepower. And Camaro's the only American car besides Corvette that offers 4-wheel disc brakes.

Camaro's got a lot more going for it, too. Like this SS version that comes with a big V8, power disc brakes, beefed-up suspension, a special floor shift and wide oval tires. And with the Rally Sport package, you've got the only sportster at its price with out-of-sight headlights.

But don't think for a minute that we won't sell you a Camaro if you're over thirty.

After all, it's not how young you are.

It's how old you aren't.

Putting you first, keeps us first.

CHEVROLET

See Olympic Gold Medalist Jean-Claude Killy, Sundays, CBS-TV. See your local TV listings.

The Camaro was revamped for 1969 with handsome all-new sheetmetal, but engine choices didn't change. SS models came with front disc brakes and racy looking (but non-functional) hood ports. A functional cowl-induction hood was an extra $79, while the hidden-headlamp Rally Sport option added $132. The 1969 Camaro was a one-year-only body style, but it ended up being a long year; production problems delayed the introduction of the redesigned 1970 models.

The 1970 Chevelle SS 454 was a definite high-water mark in the muscle car era. The solid-lifter LS6 454 was the hottest available engine, rated at a whopping 450 hp. An optional cowl induction hood drew air from the base of the windshield via a vacuum-controlled flap. Convertibles like Ray Allen's SS 454 were a rare sight at the dragstrip, since their folding top mechanisms and chassis bracing added unwanted pounds.

The all-new 1970 Camaros finally hit the streets in February 1970. Z28s packed a 360-hp LT1 350. Rally Sport-equipped models got a unique nose with a soft Endura grille surround (far left). Meanwhile, NHRA drag racing took a big step away from "stock" car racing with the creation of the new Pro Stock class. Many former Super Stock competitors, including Butch Leal and Bill "Grumpy" Jenkins, made the switch to this new, less-restrictive class.

A 1971 SS 454 could still roast the hides, but the times were quickly changing. Emissions standards had forced a switch to low-lead fuel, which in turn cut compression ratios, while insurance surcharges on supercars prompted tamer power-to-weight ratios. The top 1971 Chevelle performance engine was the hydraulic lifter, 365-hp LS5 454. For '72, the LS5 was down to 270 hp.

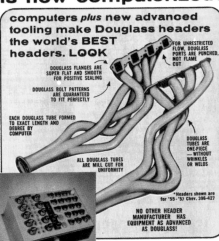

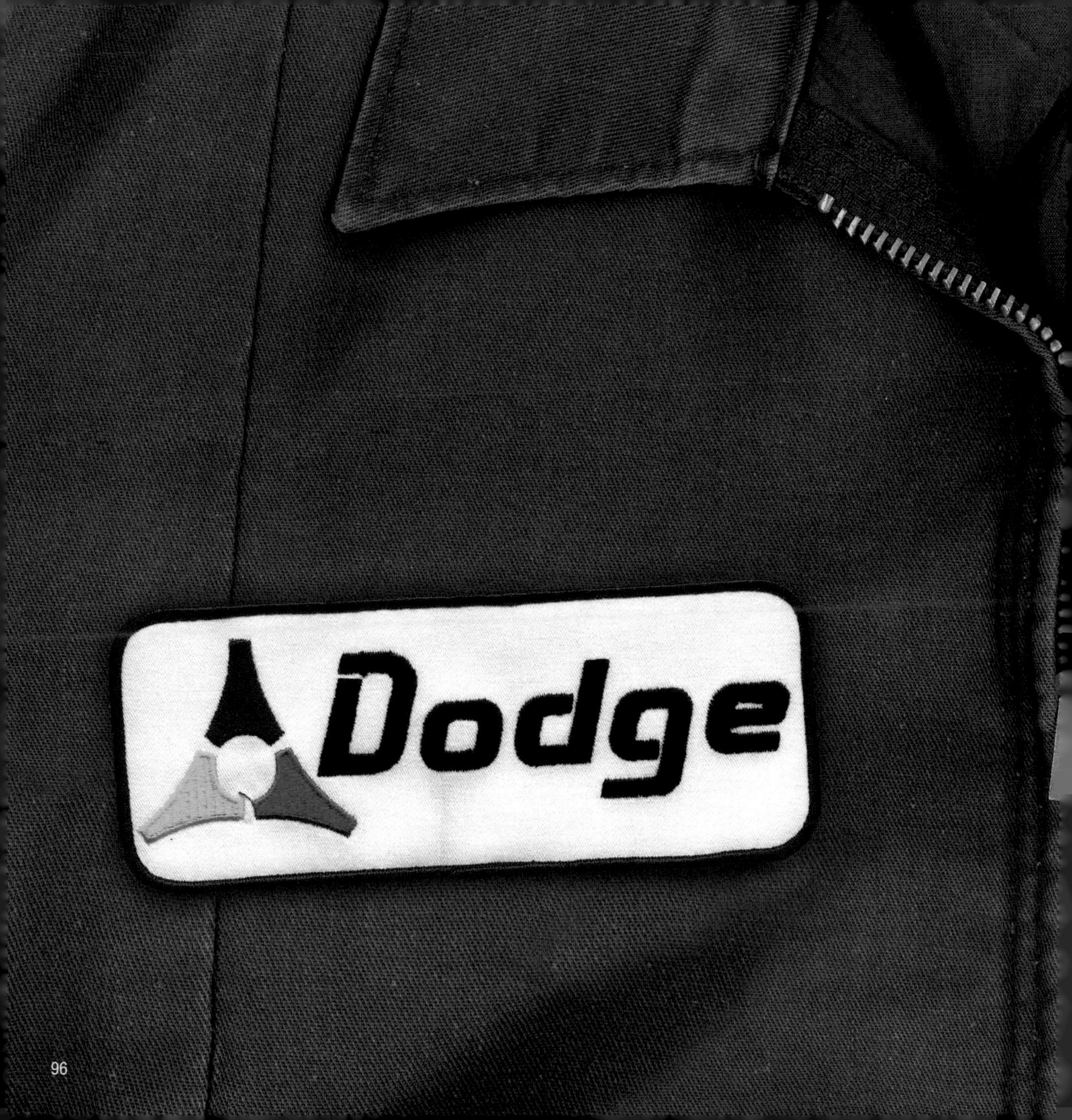
Dodge

The downsized 1962 Dodges floundered in the mainstream car market, but racers liked them for their light weight and available 410-hp "Ramcharger" 413. Polara 500s (below) were the topline models; no-frills Darts (bottom) were the budget specials. All 413s had wedge-shaped combustion chambers, but the Ramcharger was designed for "maximum" performance, hence the unofficial "Max Wedge" title. Chrysler intended it for "sanctioned acceleration trials," not for the street, but more than a few Dodges conducted "trials" away from the strip.

426 ramcharger V8!

HIGH PERFORMANCE FROM DODGE

For '63, the Ramcharger was bored out to 426 cubic inches. It made 415 hp on 11.0:1 compression, or 425 hp on 13.5:1. Note the unique upswept exhaust headers; the Dodge engine bay was too narrow to fit conventional pipes. This bare-bones 330 two-door sedan has a close-ratio three-speed floor shift, but a heavy-duty pushbutton Torqueflite was also available.

Jim Thornton and Herman Mozer (979) coming off the line in S/SA class.

Some days you win

Mozer and Al Eckstrand in final run for Top Stock Eliminator title.

Some days you lose

The fortunes on the straight and narrow warpath change as quickly as the gears in the go-box! Today you tear 'em up. Tomorrow is another day. Your machine has got to be mean . . . you've got to be good . . . and you've got to come out of the hole with more togetherness than Amos and Andy! That's the drama of the drag strip, man and machine.

That's why more than 100,000 buffs bulged the track at Indy for the NHRA's big showdown—the world championships.

And what a showdown! On Saturday, Jim Thornton in a '63 Dodge downed his Ramcharger teammate, Herman Mozer, on his

way to royalty in the Super Stock Automatic Class. Next day, running for the meet's most coveted honor—Top Stock Eliminator — Mozer turned the tables and gave Thornton the thumb. But the event was far from over. Mozer still had to face the present "Mr. Eliminator," Al Eckstrand in Lawman, another specially equipped '63 Dodge. And another winner is defeated. Mozer edged him by 1/100th of a second with an e.t. of 12.22.

Some days you win. Some days you lose. That's what keeps the quarter-mile jaunt so interesting. But have you noticed? When a Dodge loses these days . . . it's to another Dodge.

Hot Dodge

DODGE DIVISION | CHRYSLER MOTORS CORPORATION

Al Eckstrand wheeled a Ramchargers 1963 Polara to a Top Stock Eliminator at the 1963 NHRA Winternationals. His ET was 12.44 seconds at 115.08 mph. Half-and-half painted wheels were helpful in gauging wheelspin off the line. Mopars usually dominated at the strips in 1963 against the heavier competition, as Dodge made sure to point out in advertising. But Ford's lightweight Thunderbolts would have Dodge drivers looking over their shoulders in 1964 (right).

The 426-cid Ramcharger Wedge remained the top Mopar performance engine...until the debut of the soon-to-be-legendary 426 Hemi in early 1964. The new Hemi immediately propelled Dodge and Plymouth into the NASCAR winner's circle and into drag-racing dominance. The engine was a few years away from street duty, but did find a home beneath the hood of a few factory-built 330/440/Polara lightweight drag cars.

Roger Lindamood's "Color Me Gone" Dodge turned an 11.31 at 127.84 mph at the 1964 NHRA Nationals to take the Top Stock title. A few early-'64 Dodge Super Stock cars, like "Dandy Dick" Landy's, were two-door hardtops instead of the lighter two-door sedan bodies. This pair of identically prepared, factory-backed 1964 Dodges ran in the NHRA's newly created S/FX (Supercharged Factory Experimental) class. Both ran blown, fuel-injected Dodge wedge motors that put out around 900 hp.

Chrysler's corporate drag racing efforts reached extreme levels with the 1965 altered-wheelbase cars. The bizarre appearance of these radically modified production cars prompted the name "funny car." The factory photos on this page show the fiberglass body components and lightweight bumper (tipping the scales at just 80 pounds!) and a complete AWB Coronet in as-delivered form. Of course, "normal" Dodge Coronets still hit the strips as well.

Each Mopar altered wheelbase car underwent serious surgery. The axles were moved forward—the rear one by 15 inches, the front one by 10—to create a 110-inch-wheelbase racer that put about 56 percent of the car's weight over the rear tires. The steel body panels were dipped in an acid tank to make them lighter. Here, Bill Flynn's Yankee Peddler and "Dandy Dick" Landy's Coronet illustrate the benefits of all this labor—drag slick wrinkling, front wheel pulling launches. Note the towering velocity stacks on both these cars; Chrysler authorized a switch from dual four-barrel carbs to Hilborn fuel injection during the season. Note also the canvas hood tie-down straps on Landy's car...wouldn't want the hood to blow off at 140 mph.

Fastback rooflines were all the rage in the mid-Sixties, so Dodge dropped a sleek new roof on the midsize Coronet to create the 1966 Charger. Chargers also wore hidden headlamp grilles and full-width taillights. Dodge made the 426 Street Hemi available in both Coronets and Chargers; it was factory rated at 425 horsepower.

426 HEMI

Coronet changed little for 1967, but Dodge did add the R/T—for "Road and Track"—as the new muscle model. Standard were fake hood vents, a unique grille and taillamps, and the four-barrel 440 Magnum. Chargers were also little changed, but could get the 440 as an option to the base 383. The Hemi was available on both the Coronet R/T and the Charger. Here, Dick Landy's Hemi-powered Coronet R/T gets the jump on a '67 GTO.

A breathtaking, all-new Charger debuted for 1968. R/T models now came standard with a 375-hp 440, with the Hemi again optional. Psychedelic muscle car marketing wackiness was coming into full bloom. Dodge christened its performance car lineup the "Scat Pack," and rolled out a cartoon bumblebee mascot. Dick Landy's 3650-pound Hemi Charger turned a 10.86 at 127 mph. Street Chargers were good for high 13s with the Hemi, high 14s with the 440.

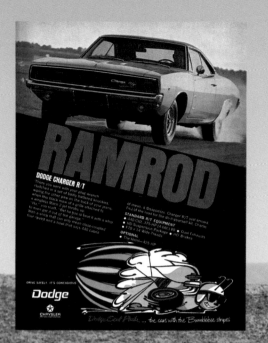

RAMROD

DODGE CHARGER R/T

There you were with your shut wrench clutched in a set of badly barbered knuckles, wiping the other paw on the back of your jeans, when the black paw on the back of your endless Mach 2 got throbs, tell... hot, oily stuff. Well be like to boat it with a whip to even get it out of the garage. With a snick that can only mean close-coupled four-speed and a howl that says 440 cubes.

of mean, it disappears. Charger R/T just arrived. Full of the good for the do-it-yourself kit. Charge.

STANDARD R/T EQUIPMENT
● 440 CID, 375-HP (4-bbl.) V8 ● Dual Exhausts
● HD Suspension Package ● HD Brakes
● F70 x 14 Wide Treads

OPTIONAL
● The Hemi— 425 HP

DRIVE SAFELY IT'S CONTAGIOUS

Dodge

CHRYSLER

Dodge Scat Pack ... the cars with the Bumblebee stripes

RUMBLE BEE

Dodge's big-bang-for-the-buck answer to Plymouth's successful Road Runner was the 1968 Super Bee, a budget version of its redesigned Coronet. Available only in a pillared coupe body style, the Super Bee came standard with a 335-hp 383, four-speed with Hurst Competition Plus shifter, heavy-duty suspension, and Charger instrumentation...all for $3037. Coronet R/T hardtops (right) started out at $3379, but came standard with the 440 Magnum.

DODGE

Dodge Scat Pack
... the cars with the Bumblebee stripes

Dodge gave its compact Dart some muscle with the late-1967 introduction of the 383-powered GTS model. For 1968, the GTS earned its stripes as a member of the Scat Pack. Rallye Suspension, bucket seats, fake hood vents, and E70x14 tires were also part of the GTS package. The 383 was still available, but a hot little 340 small block (right) was now the standard engine. Around 650 special-order Darts, like the drag car below, were built with the 375-horsepower 440.

The 1968 Hemi Darts were among the most brutal factory race cars ever built. Dodge contracted with Hurst-Campbell, Inc., to produce about 80 of these no-holds-barred drag machines. The front fenders and scooped hood were fiberglass, while the rear fenders were radiused to clear massive slicks. The heater, rear seat, and sound-deadening materials were deleted. Chrysler decreed that "All customer orders must be accompanied by a signed disclaimer indicating that the purchaser understands that this vehicle is sold without warranty and does not conform to Federal Vehicle Safety Standards."

DODGE *fever*

Dodge's Scat Pack supercars got some
minor styling changes for 1969. Super Bees
and Coronet R/Ts could now be equipped
with a Ramcharger hood, with fully functional twin scoops that could be opened and
closed by a dashboard switch. Darts got a
slightly revised grille with rectangular park-
ing lights; Chargers got a new split grille and
elongated taillights. All of the Scat Pack cars
got rectangular side marker lights and
revised tail stripes.

The muscle car era was reaching its zenith in 1969. Amidst the indulgent atmosphere were subtle reminders that lots of power can be dangerous. Beneath the far-out copy and mouthwatering standard equipment lists in Charger print advertising, Dodge inserted sober warnings such as "safety is no accident—drive with care" and "don't be caught dead wrong—drive safely."

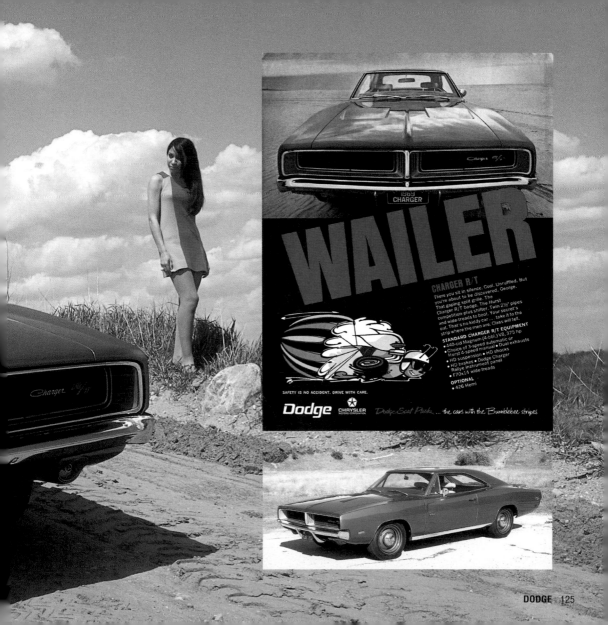

WAILER

CHARGER R/T

There you sit in silence. Cool. Unruffled. But you're about to be discovered, George. That gaping split grille. The Charger R/T badge. The Hurst competition-plus shifter. Twin 2½" pipes and wide-treads to boot. Your secret's out. That's no kiddy car ... take it to the strip where the men are. Class will tell.

STANDARD CHARGER R/T EQUIPMENT
• 440-cid Magnum (4-bbl.) V8, 375 hp
• Choice of 3-speed automatic or Hurst 4-speed manual • Dual exhausts
• HD suspension • HD shocks
• HD brakes • Dodge Charger Rallye instrument panel
• F70x14 wide-treads

OPTIONAL
• 426 Hemi

SAFETY IS NO ACCIDENT, DRIVE WITH CARE.

Dodge ⊕ CHRYSLER MOTORS CORPORATION

Dodge Scat Pack ... the cars with the Bumblebee stripes

High-profile, winning drag racers did plenty of duty as celebrity pitchmen. Dick Landy was one of the first factory backed drag racers, and had cultivated a solid image for himself by the end of the decade. His trademark was a giant cigar that he chomped (but never lit) while racing. Landy also conducted "performance seminars" at Dodge dealerships around the country, dispensing know-how to Mopar enthusiasts who were eager to wring the most performance out of their vehicles.

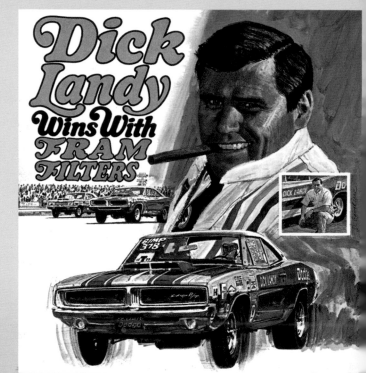

Chrysler and Ford were locked in a fierce battle for superspeedway supremacy in the late 60s. To combat the slippery fastback Fords and Mercurys, Dodge concocted the 1969 Charger 500 (above), a slicked-up Charger with a flush-mounted grille and rear window. When that didn't quite do the trick, Dodge pulled out all the stops and developed the Charger Daytona. The pointed nose cone reduced drag and enhanced downforce; the towering rear wing eliminated lift at triple-digit speeds. To make the car legal for NASCAR competition, Dodge built 505 street versions for sale to the public.

Hemi- and 440-powered Coronet R/Ts could get a "Track Pack" package that included a heavy-duty four-speed with Hurst linkage, a Dana rear axle with a 3.54:1 ratio, Sure-Grip non-slip differential, high-performance radiator, seven-blade fan, and dual-breaker distributor. The Coronet R/T still cut a fine profile, but sales slipped as the flashier Charger and cheaper Super Bee lured buyers away. Redline tires were also on their way out; most manufacturers would switch to raised white-letter tires for 1970.

Taking a cue from the low-buck successes of the Super Bee and Plymouth Road Runner, Dodge added a new budget performance model to the '69 Dart line-up: the Swinger 340. The 383 was exclusive to the GTS, but the upstart Swinger still outsold its more-expensive sibling by almost 10,000 units. Dodge got the message; the GTS was dropped for 1970.

Dodge finally got a true ponycar in 1970. The Challenger wore classic long-hood/short-deck proportions and was available with a bewildering array of options. R/T models came standard with a 335-hp 383 and a twin-scooped hood; a $97 option was the "Shaker" scoop, which mounted directly to the air cleaner and quivered through a hole in the hood. "Bumblebee" or longitudinal stripes were a no-cost R/T option.

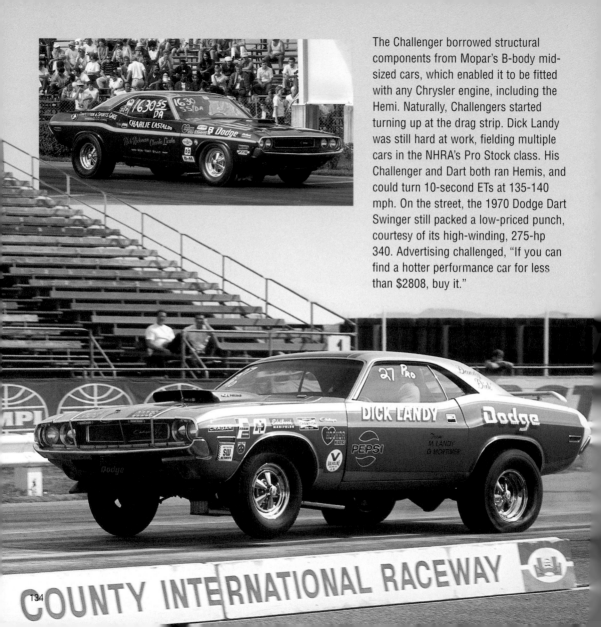

The Challenger borrowed structural components from Mopar's B-body mid-sized cars, which enabled it to be fitted with any Chrysler engine, including the Hemi. Naturally, Challengers started turning up at the drag strip. Dick Landy was still hard at work, fielding multiple cars in the NHRA's Pro Stock class. His Challenger and Dart both ran Hemis, and could turn 10-second ETs at 135-140 mph. On the street, the 1970 Dodge Dart Swinger still packed a low-priced punch, courtesy of its high-winding, 275-hp 340. Advertising challenged, "If you can find a hotter performance car for less than $2808, buy it."

COUNTY INTERNATIONAL RACEWAY

Dodge's B-body intermediates got wrap-around loop bumpers as part of their 1970 facelift. The Charger's was a simple rectangular affair; Coronets and Super Bees got a radical split bumper/grille. This 440 Six Pack-powered Super Bee wears "Plum Crazy" metallic purple paint, one of Dodge's extra-cost "High Impact" colors. Others included "Sublime" bright green, "Top Banana" yellow, and "Go-ManGo" orange.

The 1971 Demon was Dodge's version of the successful Plymouth Duster. Street Demon 340s had a 275-hp 340, but Canadian John Petrie's Pro Stocker packed a Hemi. Dodge continued to court applicants for its Scat Pack Club through brochures and magazine ads. A wallet-sized membership card, mod-design racing jacket, decals, and an illustrated tune-up tips folder were a few of the benefits of membership.

MEMBERSHIP APPLICATION

DODGE SCAT PACK CLUB

Enclosed is $5.95 for one year's membership. I understand that you will send me all the Club materials and that I will be a member in good standing of the Dodge Scat Pack Club.

Please print or type.

Name_____

Address_____

City_____ State_____ Zip_____

Age of applicant_____ Model and year of Dodge I own_____

Engine_____ Signature_____

Mail to: Scat Headquarters
P.O. Box 611
Detroit, Michigan 48221   Jacket size _____

Challengers got a revised grille and taillights for their sophomore year. R/Ts got new stripes and faux rear-fender scoops. The 383 was again standard, the 275-hp 340 and 385-hp 440 Six Pack optional. Just 71 of the 4630 R/Ts built got Hemis. The far-out colors on Billy Stepp's Pro-Stock Hemi Challenger typified the intricate, kaleidoscopic paint schemes that graced drag cars in the early Seventies. Note the screws in the outer lip of the rear wheel; these kept the sticky slicks affixed to the rims during hard launches.

PRO 330

MIAMI VALLEY
Dodge Dayton, Ohio

DRIVER Stuart McDade

SUPERCREW... PAUL FROST

SS MEMBER

LLY the KID

Firestone
Drag 500

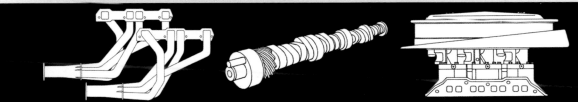

The Super Bee migrated to the voluptuous new Charger body for 1971. Dodge exclaimed, "...it looks like tomorrow and runs like it's all downhill." Both Charger R/Ts and Super Bees could have the "Ramcharger" hood, with a vacuum-operated pop-up scoop, seen here in action at the '71 NHRA U.S. Nationals. Dodge's "Hustle Stuff" catalog offered lots of hop-up parts, including Hooker headers, Iskendarian camshafts, and Six-Pack triple two-barrel induction setups.

A 1972 facelift softened the Challenger's aggressive wide-mouth look. Engine choices were much tamer as well; the Hemi was gone, and a 240-hp 340 was now the hottest Challenger mill available. The Charger made do with a 280-hp 440 four-barrel. Ad copy rationalized, "The way things are today, maybe what you need is not the world's hottest car. Maybe what you need is a well-balanced, thoroughly instrumented road machine." The Challenger would enter its last season in '74, then disappear after just four years on the market.

146

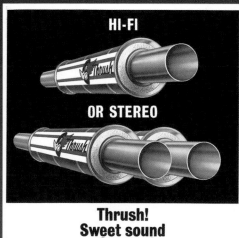

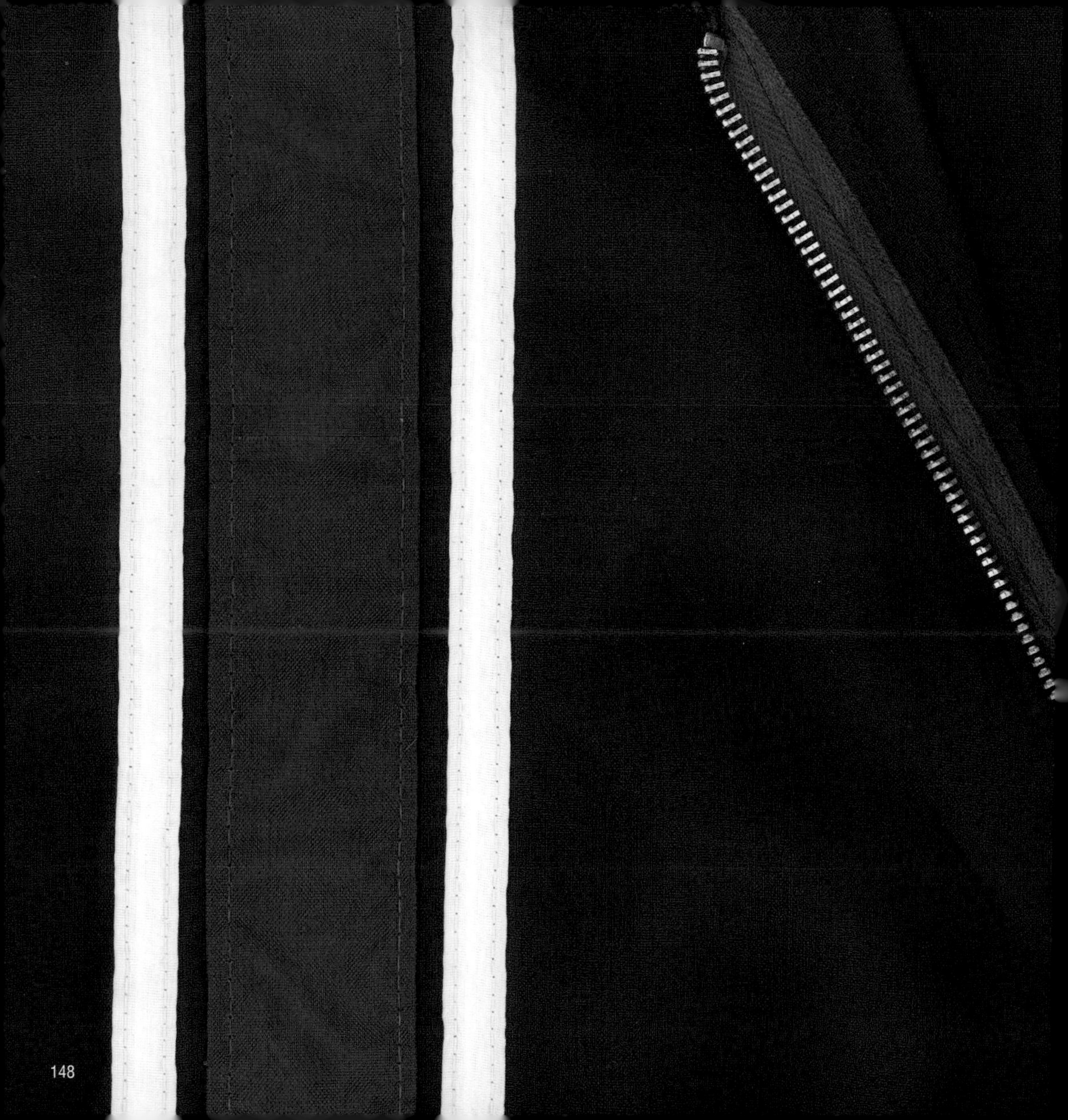

SLEEPER!

To the old carnival guessing game of "Which shell is the pea under?" you can add another—"Which Galaxie is hiding the new six-barrel?"

You can get a very precise answer, it's true, when one of these sleepers suddenly goes "zzz-z-z-ZOW!" and vanishes. But that leaves you sitting foolishly in the middle of a lot of empty landscape.

Better to know beforehand. But how? You'd think 405 horsepower, header exhausts, six-barrel carbs, 406 cubic inches and 11.4 compression couldn't be hidden. But Ford's V-8 magicians have brewed up a real street machine—no wild 2000 r.p.m. idle, no dragster noises, no battle to fire it up. Girls drive these things down to the supermarket and never suspect they are a half-throttle away from escape velocity.

Of course, you do get a clue watching one straighten out a corner. They handle! Because this engine (and the 4-barrel version) come only as a package with Heavy Duty shocks, springs, driveshaft, U-joints, brakes —plus 15-inch wheels and nylon tires. That's what makes the tab of $379.70* so fantastic—and why there are so many Galaxie sleepers around to embarrass you. But why be dominated? Get your own 406 and you won't need to guess which Galaxie has the six-barrel.

A PRODUCT OF **Ford** MOTOR COMPANY

*Manufacturer's suggested list price for extra equipment

FORD V-8

Ford answered Chevy's 409 and Chrysler's Max Wedge 413 with its first 400-plus-cid V-8. Delivered partway through the '62 model year, it was basically a Ford 390-cid V-8 bored out to 406 cubic inches. Called the Thunderbird High-Performance V-8, but available only in the new facelifted Galaxie, it signaled a fresh performance push for the blue-oval brigade.

The 406 was plenty stout, but Galaxies were still too heavy to outgun the lighter 413 Dodges and Plymouths or the new 421 Pontiacs. Here, Dick Heyler wheels his SS/SA Galaxie at the '62 Winter-nationals. A Borg-Warner T-10 four-speed was mandatory on factory-built 406 cars, but some racers found that the Cruise-O-Matic automatic was more effective in getting the power to the ground.

Galaxies gained two significant performance enhancements in mid-1963: the 427-cid V-8 and a "Sports Hardtop" semi-fastback roofline. The sleek new roof was two inches lower than the equivalent notchback and allowed a great aerodynamic advantage on NASCAR superspeedways. The strongest 427 used a pair of 652-cfm Holley four barrels for an advertised 425 hp at 6000 rpm, and 480 lb/ft of torque at 3700. The lightweight drivetrain could withstand 7000 rpm.

Even with the upgraded 427, the full-size Fords were still a bit portly. At mid-season, Ford introduced a lightweight body package for drag racers that included fiberglass front bumpers, hood, doors, and decklid, plus aluminum bumpers and brackets. Until Ford produced the minumum number of units required for an NHRA "stock" classification, the cars had to run in the A/FX class.

A precursor to the 1964 Fairlane Thunderbolt was this '63 Fairlane run by Rhode Island Ford dealer Bob Tasca. Built by Ford contractor Dearborn Steel Tubing, the one-off experimental packed a high-riser 427 and ran in the low 12s. Production Fairlanes were offered with a 271-hp version of the 289 V-8. With a four-barrel and 11.0:1 compression, it was Ford's first performance engine in a midsize car.

Ford planned to build just 50 Thunderbolts as A/FX cars but constructed 127, enough to qualify for Super/Stock, where they were very hot. Shoehorning a hefty big-block 427 into a midsize car like the Fairlane took a lot of work. Inner fenders, shock towers, suspension control arms, and springs were all modified to provide clearance for the big engine. With fiberglass doors, front body panels and bumpers, and Lexan windows, a Thunderbolt weighed just over the NHRA's 3205-pound minimum. Screened inner headlight openings routed air to the 427's dual carbs via huge air ducts.

Full-size Fords got a crisp restyle for 1964. In addition to the Thunderbolt program, Ford made another run of lightweight Galaxies for the quarter mile. All were pur- pose-built drag machines, with acid-dipped bodies and fiberglass hoods with a large "teardrop" hood scoop. The extra space was needed to clear the air cleaner on the "high-riser" 427 that lurked underhood. Slots cut into the grille helped direct cold air to the dual 780-cfm Holley four barrels.

One of history's most popular and influential cars, Mustang bowed in April 1964 with a six or a 260-cid V-8. The solid-lifter 271-hp HiPo came in June, and 2+2 fastbacks were added in the fall. Even the HiPo was little threat to true muscle cars on the street. Mustangs had more success at the strip, especially in A/FX classes, where larger engines could be used. Les Ritchey ran one of the most powerful, with Weber carbs on a SOHC 427.

Here's what can happen when you build a foundry too close to a Swiss cheese factory

You get giant holes in your intake manifold. So the only solution is to bolt eight-barrel carburetion on top and tuck a Ford 427 block underneath, and cop the title of World's Strongest Sandwich (stock division).

Seriously, this is merely a reminder that Ford doesn't stand still, even with a great engine like the 427 High Performance V-8. Peel one open now and you'll find *machined* combustion chambers, a lighter weight valve train, bigger and lighter hollow-stemmed valves, a forged steel crank with hollow crankpins, stronger con rods, pop-up pistons and a huge oil gallery low in the block (which also is new) that feeds oil directly to the main bearings.

No big engine has a right to rev the way this one does—but it does and it stays stuck together. Better still, you don't have to be an insider to get one of the good ones; this is a John Citizen engine. It goes the way it goes right off the showroom floor.

As always, Ford wraps this one up with heavy-duty springs, shocks, wheels and tires to match. That's just good sense, but it also makes an unbeatable combination. If you want to know how a vegetarian feels the day he discovers steak, just try it! Some sandwich!

Best year yet to go Ford!!
Test Drive Total Performance '65

FORD

MUSTANG · FALCON · FAIRLANE
FORD · THUNDERBIRD

PRODUCTS OF *Ford*

Ford's corporate drag racing efforts had shifted almost entirely to A/FX Mustangs by 1965, but a few competitors still flogged full-size Fords at the strip. The NHRA's factory experimental division contained A/FX, B/FX, and C/FX classes, each determined by total car weight divided by total cubic inches of engine displacement. A small-block 289 put this Galaxie 500 in the C/FX class.

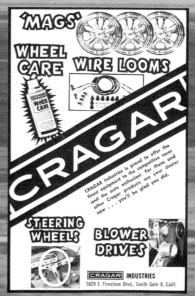

HOW TO COOK A TIGER

Take one part 335 HP V-8. Chrome plate the rocker covers, oil filler
cap, radiator cap, air cleaner cover and dip stick.

Blend high lift cam; bigger carburetor.

Mix in the new 2-way, 3-speed GTA Sport Shift that you can use either
manually or let shift itself.

Place the new shift selector between great bucket seats.

Now put on competition type springs and shocks.

Add a heavy-duty stabilizer bar.

Place over low profile 7.75 nylon whitewalls.

Touch off with distinctive GTA medallion and
contrasting racing stripe.

Cover with hardtop or 5-ply vinyl convertible top with glass
rear window. Serve in any of 15 colors.

This is the new Fairlane GTA. An original Ford recipe that may
be tasted at your Ford Dealers . . . Remember--it's a very hot dish!

FAIRLANE

GTA

A PRODUCT OF

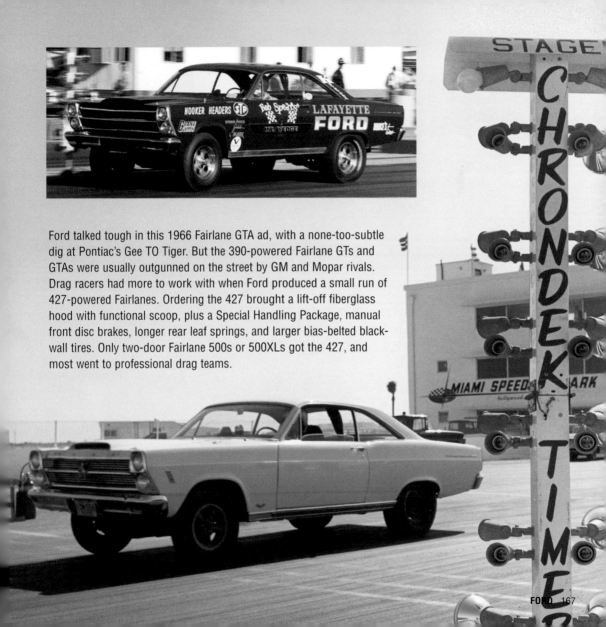

Ford talked tough in this 1966 Fairlane GTA ad, with a none-too-subtle dig at Pontiac's Gee TO Tiger. But the 390-powered Fairlane GTs and GTAs were usually outgunned on the street by GM and Mopar rivals. Drag racers had more to work with when Ford produced a small run of 427-powered Fairlanes. Ordering the 427 brought a lift-off fiberglass hood with functional scoop, plus a Special Handling Package, manual front disc brakes, longer rear leaf springs, and larger bias-belted black-wall tires. Only two-door Fairlane 500s or 500XLs got the 427, and most went to professional drag teams.

The small "S.O.H.C." lettering on the front fenders of Mike Schmitt's '66 Galaxie indicate that it is equipped with Ford's exotic SOHC 427 engine. Ford developed this single-overhead-cam motor to compete against Chrysler's dominant Hemis in stock-car racing, but NASCAR banned the "cammer" from competition. So Ford took the engine drag racing instead, using it in a run of drag-only Mustangs in 1965. Even in the heavy Galaxie chassis, the Cammer was strong enough to propel Schmitt to a '66 NHRA Winternationals Street class win with an 11.85 ET at 119.6 mph.

DESERT MOTORS INC.
RIDGECREST, CALIF.

SHOW YOUR STRIPES!

There's a lot of GT in every Fairlane.

A lot of GT spirit, luxury, and especially performance. Proof: In Union/Pure Oil Performance Trials, Fairlane took first in its class in a combined test of acceleration, braking, and gas economy. A specially prepared Fairlane won the Daytona 500. Pick your Fairlane—hardtop, convertible, sedan or wagon—and show your stripes! **FAIRLANE**

The 427 Fairlane...

is also available without numbers.

More and more people who take their driving seriously are turning to the 427 Fairlane. Some of them, like Parnelli Jones and Mario Andretti, go to the trouble of adding personalized touches — such as numbers 18 inches tall!

That's Mr. Jones' 427 Fairlane above, after a Sunday drive that began and ended at Riverside, California recently. Mr. Andretti likes to go Fairlaning near Daytona, Florida. Before you go to the line next Sunday take a good look at your equipment. If you're serious about your driving, try a real serious car ... the 427 cubic inch Fairlane.

This machine produces a no-nonsense 425 horsepower, and a sincere 480 foot-pounds of torque at 3700 revolutions per minute. If you want to add numbers ... go ahead. But, remember, you'll have to give every kid on the block from 8 to 80 a ride!

Fairlanes got mildly revised grilles and trim for 1967. The 427 became a regular production option, but fewer than 200 are believed to have been built. The solid-lifter mill had 410 hp with a single four-barrel or 425 with dual quads. Only base, 500, or 500XL Fairlanes could get the 427; GTs stuck with two- and four-barrel 390s, the latter down by 15 hp, to 320. Parnelli Jones' Fairlane took the checkered flag at the 1967 Riverside 500. Weeks later, Mario Andretti drove a Fairlane to his first and only NASCAR victory at the '67 Daytona 500.

Ford required buyers of 1967 427 Fairlanes to sign a disclaimer that outlined the special characteristics of the high-performance engine. It stated in part, "Engine noise will be objectionable due to increased piston clearance and mechanical valve tappet clearance" and "A vehicle equipped with the high-performance engine is designed for competition and is expected to bc used for such purposes. The standard vehicle warranty coverage will not apply, and the special warranty provisions applying to vehicles equipped with high performance engines are to be explained by the selling dealer."

The Fairlane was completely restyled for 1968, with the top series renamed Torino. A sleek new fastback body style was available in Fairlane 500, Torino, or Torino GT trim. GT fastbacks got bodyside "C-stripes," bucket seats, and styled steel wheels. The 427 was the top engine option at the beginning of the model year, but it was later replaced by the 428 Cobra Jet. Former moonshine runner Hubert Platt ran a variety of drag machines throughout the Sixties under the "Georgia Shaker" monicker. His Super Stock/F Automatic Torino was an 11.9-12.0-second car.

Street Mustangs gained big-block power in 1967 when the 335-hp 390 V-8 was added to the GT options list. The '68s got revised grilles and trim, plus "C-stripes" that wrapped around the bodyside coves. Steve McQueen thrashed a Highland Green 390-powered GT through the streets of San Francisco in the movie *Bullitt*. McQueen's mount was modified with American Torq-Thrust mags, removed trim, and a beefed-up engine and suspension.

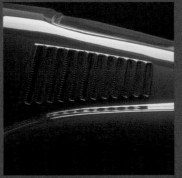

The 390 was a step-up from the small-block 289, but Mustangs still didn't have the giddyup to out-pace the big-block competition. That changed in April 1968, when Ford introduced the 428 Cobra Jet. The first batch were white, lightweight fast-backs, built to meet the NHRA's production mini-mum. The Cobra Jet was based on the staid 428 big-car motor, but had competition-brewed 427 V-8 heads, a 735-cfm Holley four barrel, and ram-air induction. Factory backed 428 CJs dominated their class at the 1968 NHRA Winternationals.

Ford jumped on the budget muscle bandwagon with the '69 Fairlane Cobra. It was a dressed-down Torino with a blacked-out grille, plain bench seat, and the 428 Cobra Jet engine. Base price was a reasonable $3200, but the lengthy options list included such temptations as a limited-slip differential ($63), power steering ($100), power front disc brakes ($65), bucket seats with console ($169), 8000-rpm tach ($48), and Ram Air ($133). Early-production Cobras carried multicolored decals of a stylized snake with fangs bared and tires trailing flames; later cars had the metal emblems shown here.

COBRA

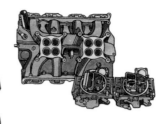

Fairlane Cobras also came in "SportsRoof" fastback form. They weighed about 60 pounds more than their hardtop siblings, but buyers liked their sleeker look. The aerodynamic fastback shape might have helped a little at the strip, but it was a huge advantage at the high-banked superspeedways of NASCAR racing. Ford's catalog of over-the-counter performance parts included plenty of go-fast goodies, such as stronger crankshafts, high-compression pistons and Cobra Jet connecting rods, medium-riser dual-quad intake manifolds, and Cobra Jet cylinder heads with chromed-stemmed valves.

Mustangs got got longer, lower, and swoopier in a stem-to-stern 1969 redesign. Side stripes, a flat black hood with available "Shaker" scoop, and styled steel wheels distinguished the new-for-'69 Mach 1 fastback. Ford's new 351 V-8 was standard, but the potent Cobra Jet was optional. Ford also introduced two racing-inspired Boss Mustangs. Boss 302 was the street version of Ford's SCCA Trans Am race cars. Boss 429 enabled Ford to qualify an exotic "semi-hemi" V-8 for NASCAR racing. The Boss 302 and Boss 429 engines had their charms, but the Cobra Jet was still the weapon of choice for serious drag racing. Hubert Platt headed up the Eastern Ford Drag Team with a CJ-powered Super Stock 'Stang.

Hot Mustangs were usually based on the sleek fastback models, but the coupes were actually a bit lighter. Here, Jerry Baker launches the Polaris drag team Pro-Stocker at the 1971 Winternationals. Detroit Locker "No-Spin" rear ends used a locking gear-type differential for serious traction.

New shape of muscle for '70.

Torinos got a shapely new body for 1970. Cobra models returned, but now packed a standard 360-hp 429. Ordering the Drag Pack with the Cobra engine added Traction-Lok 3.91:1 or Detroit Locker 4:30:1 gears, a mechanical-lifter cam, oil cooler, forged aluminum pistons, four-bolt mains, and a 780-cfm four-barrel, for a 375 hp rating. Torino GTs could have a four-barrel 351 with 300 hp, while the 290-hp "Boss" 302 was reserved for the Boss 302 Mustang.

429-SCJ

351-4V

Boss 302-4V

PRE-STAGED

STAGED

The Mustang grew longer, wider, and up to 600 pounds heavier for 1971. SportsRoof models had radical fastback styling that looked great, but wreaked havoc with rearward visibility. The Boss 351 was the quickest and most roadable 'Stang in the stable. Its High-Output 351 delivered a solid 330 hp and sub-6-second 0-60 times.

Equipped with Genuine Fenton "HAWK" Wheels

Practically Everyone Prefers Fenton Stick Shifts

Mercury introduced the Super Marauder 427 in 1963. In base form, a 780-cfm Holley four-barrel was mounted atop an aluminum intake manifold to produce 410 hp and 476 lb-ft of torque. An additional $461.60 bought twin 780-cfm Holleys and 11.5:1 compression. This setup was good for 425 hp and 480 lb-ft of torque.

**The price
is medium...
the action
maximum...
the car is
Mercury**

Full-size Mercurys got an attractive pointed nose with an "electric shaver" grille and oblong taillights for 1964. A floor-mounted four-speed was mandatory when the dual-quad 427 was ordered; just 42 Marauders were so equipped. Famed racer Parnelli Jones wheeled 427-powered Marauders to first-place finishes at the Pikes Peak hill climbs in both 1963 and '64.

Mercury

Marauder

Pikes Peak Champion

In '64, Mercury began a serious assault on the nation's dragstrips with a run of specially built Comets. All 11 cars (ten coupes and one station wagon) were powered by the "Hi-Riser" 427, which dynoed at over 500 hp. Mercury snagged top Chevy racers "Dyno" Don Nicholson and Ronnie Sox after GM enacted a company-wide ban on corporate-sponsored racing activities in 1963.

A PRODUCT OF *Ford* MOTOR COMPANY · LINCOLN-MERCURY DIVISION

Comet Drag Team, front view.

(out of consideration for competitors who will become very familiar with the rear view)

Arnie "The Farmer" Beswick, "Dyno" Don Nicholson, and Hayden Proffitt pose next to their SOHC 427-powered 1965 Comets and enjoy a staged victory toast in these magazine ad photos. Nicholson stayed with Mercury for the rest of the muscle car era, but Beswick and Proffitt would return to GM cars. Midway through the season, Ford released a Hilborn injection unit, seen at right on "Fast" Eddie Schartman's ride.

Mercury **Comet**
the world's 100,000-mile durability champion

CYCLONE GT

Comet graduated to the larger Fairlane platform for 1966. Advertising for the sporty new Cyclone GT model focused heavily on drag racing and performance. The SOHC 427 (above) was used in Mercury's drag-only machines; the engine shown produced over 600 hp on gasoline. Street Comet GTs got a 335-hp 390.

LINCOLN-MERCURY DIVISION OF Ford

Comets got a new grille and other trim changes for '67. The hood scoops on regular-production Cyclone GTs were for looks only, but this 427-powered Cyclone's were functional. Cyclone sales sputtered as Mercury hot car buyers were lured by the new-for-'67 Cougar. Only 3797 GTs were built.

A new Montego nameplate graced Mercury's intermediates, with the 428 CJ Cyclone GT atop the line. *Motor Trend*'s turned a 13.8 at 101.6 with 4.11:1 gears, automatic, and the Traction-Lok differential. SportsRoof fastback models (below left) vastly outsold their notchback counterparts (below right). Racing legend Dan Gurney drove a Cougar in the 1967 Trans Am season. For 1968, Mercury produced a limited-edition Cougar XR-7G model, seen here with Gurney himself. The package included special badges, fiberglass hood scoop, and available power sunroof. The aluminum "Rader" wheels on this prototype were later recalled for cracking and sealing problems and replaced with styled steel wheels.

Mercury has the word for a new performance scene.

make it with these 1969 "sweet streepers" from Mercury

sure footed cat
Cougar 351-4V

scene stealer
Marauder X-100

streep sweeper
Cyclone C.J.

the prowler
Cougar C.J. 428

GROOVE

"They move. They groove. They corner and haul it. They're StreepCars. Maxi-performance machines for Mini-E.T.'s, crisp cornering, startling speed. StreepCars make every scene." Thus spake Mercury of its 1969 performance car lineup. "Streep" stood for street and strip. Pictured above is a sample of the over-the-counter hop-ups available through Mercury dealers. They included headers and free-flow exhausts, deep-sump oil pan, special intake manifolds, dual quads, low-restriction air cleaners, even a multi-carb Weber setup.

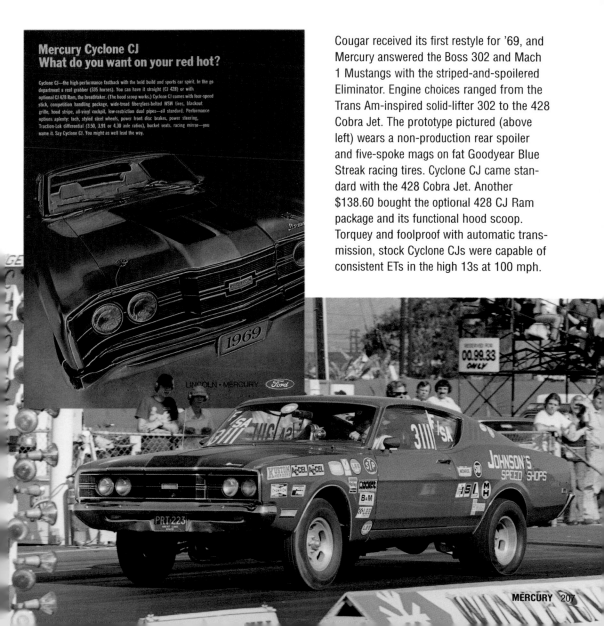

Cougar received its first restyle for '69, and Mercury answered the Boss 302 and Mach 1 Mustangs with the striped-and-spoilered Eliminator. Engine choices ranged from the Trans Am-inspired solid-lifter 302 to the 428 Cobra Jet. The prototype pictured (above left) wears a non-production rear spoiler and five-spoke mags on fat Goodyear Blue Streak racing tires. Cyclone CJ came standard with the 428 Cobra Jet. Another $138.60 bought the optional 428 CJ Ram package and its functional hood scoop. Torquey and foolproof with automatic transmission, stock Cyclone CJs were capable of consistent ETs in the high 13s at 100 mph.

The Eliminator package entered its second and last year on the mildly restyled Cougar. Standard Eliminator color choices consisted of Pastel Blue or Competition Orange, Yellow, Blue, Gold, and Green. Mercury's Competition colors matched Ford's Grabber colors. A 300-hp 351 was standard, the 290-hp Boss 302 or 335-hp 428 Cobra Jet optional. The Hurst T-handle lever provided a better grip during power shifts. Mercury dealers offered Autolite Staged Performance engine upgrade kits in three levels: Impressor, Controller, and Dominator. The Boss 429 engine was listed as an option, but only two are believed to have been installed. One was in "Fast" Eddie Schartman's drag car. Note the Lakewood "Traction Action" bars visible in front of the rear slicks. These "slapper bars" prevented excessive leaf spring flexing and helped prevent wheel hop for better traction.

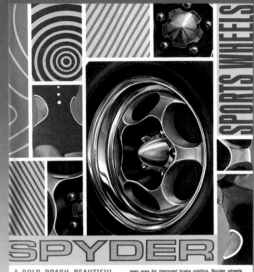

Cyclone GT. Password for action in the 70's.
The streeter that looks like a racing car.

New, sophisticated Cyclone GT. Mercury's great street machine for driving men on both sides of age thirty. With thrusting, scooped hood. Concealed headlamps. Hi-back buckets. Competition Handling Package. F70 x 14 traction belted tires. 351 V-8. All standard.

This side of thirty? Heavy it up with the thundering Super CJ 429 V-8 (375 horsepower) and 4-speed with Hurst Shifter®. That side of thirty? Do the same. Cyclone GT will set you free. Want more? See your Lincoln-Mercury dealer for our high-performance catalog.

'70 Mercury Cyclone GT

MERCURY CYCLONE — Ford

Cyclone GTs and Spoilers were Mercury's top performance intermediates for 1970. Spoiler's $3759 base price included a 370-hp Ram Air 429, four-speed with Hurst T-handle, 3:50.1 Traction-Lok, competition handling package, and G70x14 tires. The Drag Pack option gave the 429 solid lifters, stronger internals, and 375 hp. Just 1631 Spoilers were built.

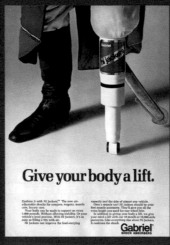

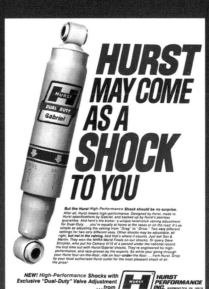
213

Police needed it... Olds built it... Pursuit proved it!
Put this one on <u>your</u> WANTED list!

OLDSMOBILE 4-4-2

4-BARREL CARBURETOR!
4-ON-THE-FLOOR!
DUAL EXHAUSTS!

Now ready to put more muscle and hustle into *your* everyday performance needs! The Olds *4-4-2* —brand new action-tailored F-85 package—delivers 310 h.p. and 355 lb.-ft. of torque from its 4-barrel Jetfire Rocket V-8! Makes life still more exciting with a floor-mounted 4-speed synchro-mesh transmission, track-tested Red-Line tires, dual exhausts and heavy-duty chassis com-ponents—all part of the package!* Ask for details on the all-new *4-4-2*—available in any F-85 V-8 model except station wagons.

Additional special-duty options also available at extra cost.

GET THE FULL STORY!
See your
Local Authorized Oldsmobile
Quality Dealer!

GO OLDS *WHERE THE ACTION IS!*

OLDSMOBILE DIVISION · GENERAL MOTORS CORPORATION · QUALITY BUILDERS OF THE NINETY-EIGHT, STARFIRE, SUPER 88, DYNAMIC 88, JETSTAR I, JETSTAR 88, F-85

OLDS 442

Oldsmobile's first "muscle car" since its 1949 Rocket 88 was a police-package option group for the '64 F-85/Cutlass series (left). Called 4-4-2, it came with a 310-hp 330-cid V-8 and stood for four-barrel carb, four-speed manual, and dual exhausts. Right: The '65s got a 345-hp V-8 to redefine 4-4-2 as 400 cid, four-barrel carb, dual exhausts. These turned 15s at 98 mph.

By its third year, the 4-4-2 had become the benchmark for balanced muscle-car performance. No rival handled or stopped better, and with up to 360 hp and factory-available forced-air induction and Hurst shifters, few could ignore it in a straight line. The car's new-for-'66 body was the basis for one of the era's wildest exhibition drag cars, the Hurst Hairy Olds. It used two supercharged 425-cid Toronado V-8s driving all four wheels and hit 170 mph in the quarter. The 4-4-2 was a fine runner in the tamer stock-class categories, too.

keeper of the cool

...was the 1967 advertising tag line for the 4-4-2's W-30 Forced-Air-Induction System. The $300 dealer-installed option put discrete engine-air intakes above and below the front parking lights. It was more efficient than rivals' hood scoops, and brought internal engine mods, but carried the same 350-hp rating as other 4-4-2s.

A curvaceous '68 redesign for midsize Oldsmobiles agreed with the 4-4-2's classy image. Induction scoops now were below the front bumper, and W-30 editions had 360 hp, good for 13.3s at 103 mph. A factory linkup netted the limited-edition Hurst/Olds. It packed a 390-hp 455 Toronado V-8 and special silver paint. And the '60s hippest comedy act showed it was no drag by fielding this quarter-miler.

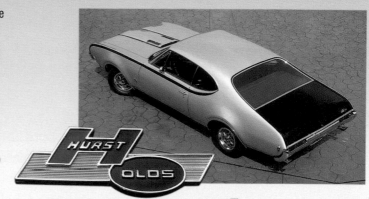

DR. OLDSMOBILE CREATES A 1969 W·MACHINE. OR TWO.

The advertising fantasy of a mad scientist conjuring ever-more-potent muscle cars put Olds in tune with the times for '69. Dr. Oldsmobile and his minions hawked the W-30 4-4-2's under-bumper air-induction, blueprinted 360-hp 400-cid V-8, and heavy-duty gear sets. They also brewed up the new W-31 package for the lower-cost Cutlass S and F-85 models. Pitched as an insurance-beater, it put air induction on a 325-hp 350-cid V-8.

226

The Hurst/Olds shed any sense of decorum for '69. "Firefrost Gold" striping accented its white paint, its trunklid sprouted an air foil, and its hood got a dual-snout scoop said to be more efficient than Olds' under-bumper air inlets. At 380 hp, the 455 V-8 was down 10 hp from '68. A performance-modified automatic with Hurst Dual-Gate shifter was again the sole transmission. These cars cost $4180, weighted 3970 pounds and turned low 14s at 101 mph. Just 912 were built. Berejik-backed Oldsmobiles set 10 national drag records and were effective billboards.

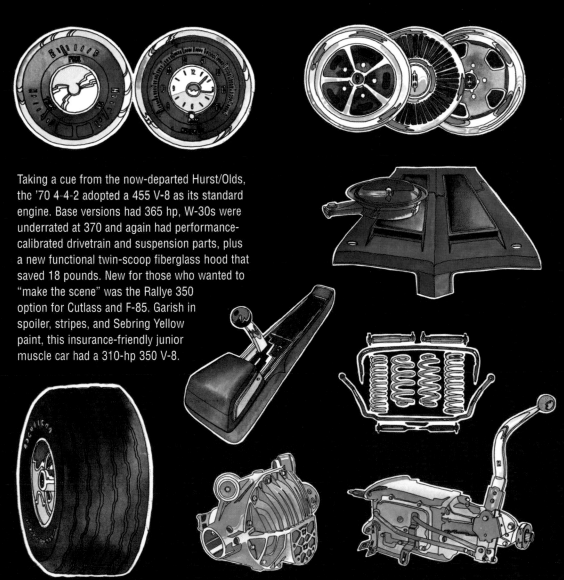

Taking a cue from the now-departed Hurst/Olds, the '70 4-4-2 adopted a 455 V-8 as its standard engine. Base versions had 365 hp, W-30s were underrated at 370 and again had performance-calibrated drivetrain and suspension parts, plus a new functional twin-scoop fiberglass hood that saved 18 pounds. New for those who wanted to "make the scene" was the Rallye 350 option for Cutlass and F-85. Garish in spoiler, stripes, and Sebring Yellow paint, this insurance-friendly junior muscle car had a 310-hp 350 V-8.

"Wouldn't it be nice to have an Escape Machine?" was an Olds ad slogan put to fine use by this '70 stock-class dragger. On the street, where muscle reputations were really made, a 4-4-2 could be over-looked amid the Chevelles, Chargers, and 'Cudas. But serious rivals knew the score. Off the showroom floor, a 4-4-2 packed 500 lbs/ft of torque and could have factory-spec 5.00:1 gears. W-30s got trick stuff like a factory blueprinted mill, plastic fender liners, and an alu-minum differential housing. Overlook one of those at your peril.

Above: GM detuned its engines for '71, and shelved gross horsepower ratings for net, a truer reflection of output. The 4-4-2's 455 now had 270 hp net (340 gross). W-30s had 300 (350 gross), but were still strong at 14.8 and 98 mph in the quarter. Right: With factory-bred muscle on the wane, Olds relied on Hurst Performance, Inc. to carry its banner, and Hurst/Olds models would be offered through 1984. The '72 Cutlass Supreme-based version restarted the partnership. It had a 455 in base or W-30 tune, and Hurst paint and trim. A Hurst power sunroof was a coupe option. The convertible was the basis for the '72 Indy 500 Pace Car, and Olds offered both body styles as production pace car replicas.

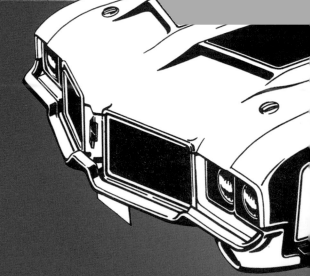

OFFICIAL PACE CAR

TACHS

not
just
another,
but a...

better tach from TELEFLEX

NOW SOMETHING NEW FROM

**df TACHOMETER FOR THE ULTIMATE IN
PERFORMANCE — THE 10 GRAND MODEL #3-250-10**

3-TRANSISTOR UNIT / NEW TAUT BAND METER /
ACCURATE WITHIN ½ OF 1% / 250° OF SCALE
LENGTH / CALIBRATED FOR 0-10,000 RPM / ADJUSTABLE FOR 6 OR 8 CYLINDER ENGINES / INTER-
NALLY ILLUMINATED DIAL / DRAWS ONLY 2% CURRENT OF EXISTING TACHOMETERS / TACH HAS
NO EFFECT ON PERFORMANCE OF YOUR ENGINE / REQUIRES NO SENDING UNIT

**df TACHOMETER
CUSTOM 8 #2-100-8**

A TWO-TRANSISTOR UNIT /
ACCURATE WITHIN 1% / PIVOT-
AND-JEWEL METER / 100° OF SCALE
LENGTH / OPERATES ON 6 OR 12
VOLT SYSTEMS / 6 OR 8 CYLINDER
ENGINES / REQUIRES NO SENDING
UNIT / RECOMMENDED FOR HIGH
RPM ENGINES

**3
MODELS
TO CHOOSE
FROM

ONE
IS RIGHT
FOR
YOU**

**df TACHOMETER
STANDARD 8 #1-100-8**

A ONE-TRANSISTOR UNIT /
ACCURATE WITHIN 1% / PIVOT-
AND-JEWEL METER / 100° OF SCALE
LENGTH / OPERATES ON 6 OR 12
VOLT SYSTEMS / 6 OR 8 CYLINDER
ENGINES / REQUIRES NO SENDING
UNIT / NOT RECOMMENDED FOR
HIGH RPM ENGINES

QUALITY

df

DEPENDABILITY

df DRAG FAST
7417 4TH AVE. SO., SEATTLE, WASH. 98108

PLEASE SEND: CATALOG & DECAL FOR 50¢
NAME_____
ADDRESS_____
CITY_____STATE_____

DIXCO announces HT/x

FOR THE COMMAND POSITION

Sleek, low and commanding describes the HT/x . . .
the Tachometer that mounts up front in the command position.

HT/x gets you off the line faster by keeping your eyes on
the road or track while you monitor RPM's at the same time.

Designed for a pretty racy crowd, HT/x features: Adjustable
RPM set pointer • Illuminated 200° scale • Shock,
weather, and theft protection • Precision Electric
Meter • Mounts with one ¾" hole in hood
• Installs in minutes.

HT/x . . . It's the going thing, see it at your dealers today.

DIXCO

100% ALL AMERICAN, FROM THE LEADER DIXSON, INC. GRAND JUNCTION, COLO. FULLY GUARANTEED

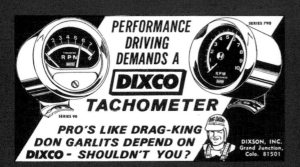

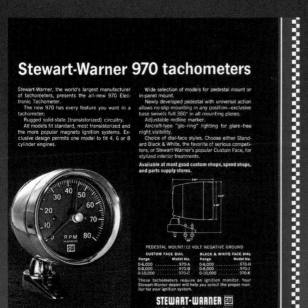

Like their Dodge counterparts, Plymouth's full-size models were downsized for '62, gaining some peculiar styling, but losing up to 400 pounds of speed-robbing curb weight. Combine that with the newly fortified 400-plus horsepower 413-cid V-8, and you had a threat to anything on wheels. Plymouth called its version of this engine the Super Stock 413, and many went into unassuming two-door sedans like this bare-bones Belvedere. This is pure Mopar muscle.

Full-size Dodges returned to a 119-inch wheelbase for '63, but Plymouth stuck with the 116-inch span. Both divisions cleaned up their styling. The hot new engine was the 426 Wedge, basically a bored 413. It had dual quads, lovely "rams-horn" headers, and up to 425 hp. In a Belvedere properly set up for street (above) or strip (below), it could run a sub-13-second quarter mile.

The 426 Wedge powered Dodges and Plymouths to eight NHRA records in 1963. Teams running the mill were a force nationwide, and here are two of Plymouth's more-popular Super Stock crews. Detroit's "Golden Commando" cars included this SS/Automatic, which employed Mopar's dash-mounted transmission pushbuttons. Tom Grove's Union City, California-based "Melrose Missile III" was a West Coast winner. At left, he takes on Bill Hanyon's Fury at the '63 Winternationals. Manual versions of these cars used a three-speed; Chrysler did yet have a four-speed.

1964

Chrysler revived its mighty Hemi V-8 for '64, unveiling it at Daytona in February 1964. It promptly swept the first three places in NASCAR's biggest event. The Hemi-powered No. 43 Plymouth of winner Richard Petty featured prominently in post-race promotions. Rated a maximum 425 hp but actually making around 570, the 426-cid Hemi (below) was reserved exclusively for competition cars in '64. Non-race '64 Plymouths showed off their cleaner new styling, and packed a solid punch of their own when ordered with a revised 426 V-8 of conventional design called the Street Wedge. It was offered in three states of tune: 365, 414, and 425 hp.

NASCAR Hemis used one four-barrel carb. Drag versions had dual quads, and since the mill wasn't a regular-production piece, the first Plymouths and Dodges to run them slotted into NHRA's Factory Experimental class. Super Stock was the province of the 426 Wedges, often seen in factory lightweight cars. Here Bill Shirely in "Golden Commando #4" and Bill Hanyon aboard the Milne Brothers Plymouth charge the Pomona strip at the '64 Winternationials. These wedges ran mid-11s at 115-118 mph.

Did you know

that the 1965 Plymouth Barracuda
has an optional Formula 'S' sports package
that includes a Commando 273-cu.-in.
V-8 engine*; heavy-duty shocks, springs, and
sway bar; a tachometer; wide-rim (14-in.)
wheels, special Blue Streak tires, and
simulated bolt-on wheel covers?

You do now.

THE ROARING '65s
FURY
BELVEDERE
VALIANT
BARRACUDA
Plymouth

*The Commando 273 engine has a 4-barrel carburetor;
10.5:1 compression ratio; high-lift, high-overlap cam;
dome-top pistons; dual breaker points; solid lifters;
special intake system with unsilenced air cleaner;
low back-pressure exhaust system with exposed resonators
and an engine dress-up package.

PLYMOUTH DIVISION ✦ CHRYSLER
MOTORS CORPORATION

Barracuda was the top-selling '65 Plymouth. Formula
S versions had 235 hp; they handled well, but were
tepid in a straight line. The Hemi was still competition-
only for 1965, and made for some wild fish. Above,
Richard Petty dragged one during NASCAR's brief ban
of the engine from its tracks. Below, Tom "Mongoose"
McEwen's car mounted its Hemi behind the front seat.

Pro drag racing was one of the few big-time sports in which women competed head-to-head with men. Among the best was "Drag-On-Lady" Shirley Shahan, a 27-year-old California clerical worker who took up drag racing while dating her husband-to-be, racer H.L. Shahan. She set a Super Stock/Automatic record of 127.30 mph and turned an 11.21-second ET in her Hemi Belvedere.

It started in '64 with wheels moved forward just 3-4 inches to offset the heavy Hemi V-8. By '65, the "funny" business had blossomed into Mopar's radical altered-wheelbase program. The factory built 12 of these drag-only specials, split evenly between Plymouth and Dodge. Wheels shifted ahead as much as 15 inches and feather-light body panels put more than half the car's weight on the rear tires. Velocity stacks identified Hemis running fuel injection; they turned low-9s at over 140 mph.

Hemi fans got their wish for '66 when Chrysler tamed its famous race engine enough to release it as the Street Hemi. Plymouth's showcase was its top-line midsize, the Satellite (top photos). The 425-hp 426-cid mill was a $908 option for the $2695 Satellite hardtop and was good for 0-60 mph in 5.3 seconds, the quarter in 13.8 at 104 mph. Some Hemi racers favored the lighter Belvedere two-door sedan; it turned 12s at 120.

Mopar's mainstay performance V-8 of the day was the durable 325-hp 383 (left). Big news for '67 was the Satellite-based GTX (right), counterpart to Dodge's new Coronet R/T and the first Plymouth to be marketed as a complete muscle package. Its standard engine was the 375-hp Super Commando 440 (above), good for 0-60 in about 6.5 seconds, the quarter in the low 15s. Sole GTX engine option, at $546, was the Street Hemi (below).

They don't call it King Kong for nothing.

Not hardly. A car doesn't get a name like that on looks alone. Not when it walks off with Top Stock Eliminator at the '66 Springnationals, Winternationals, Summernationals and World Championship Finals. Not when it idles like this one does. Not when it turns 11-second ETs and makes the trip sounding like—well—just ask the guy up there holding his ears.

This, you see, is a Hemi-powered Belvedere. More specifically, a Belvedere GTX. The Hemi part costs extra, and the car itself is specially set up for drag racing. But impressive? Man, it's devastating!

Your next question should be: *Do we build a street version of the GTX? With maybe just a little less hair?*

Glad you asked. We do indeed, and it comes with our 440 cu. in. (375 hp.) wedge-head as standard equipment. It also comes with a special heavy-duty suspension, hood scoops, Red Streak tires, wide rims, bigger brakes, low-restriction exhausts and a heavy-duty TorqueFlite automatic—again, it's all standard.

And if you order it with the 4-speed, you get coarse-pitch "Hemi" gears, a heavy-duty rear axle, viscous-drive fan, unsilenced air cleaner and a dual-point distributor as part of the bargain. Sound King-Kongish, too? It is. Because Plymouth is out to win you over. **'67 Belvedere GTX**

 *Plymouth*   CHRYSLER MOTORS CORPORATION

GTX's $3350 base price included TorqueFlite three-speed automatic (four-speed manual optional), beefed suspension, and upgraded drum brakes (front discs optional). Also standard: bucket seats, stripes, and dummy hood scoops—though the one above has a factory-developed, dealer-installed functional fresh-air hood. Just 720 of 11,396 GTXs made for '67 were ordered with the 426 Hemi. Factory-backed Ronnie Sox was a top ambassador of Plymouth performance.

WHY RONNIE SOX FEEDS "THE BOSS" THROUGH CARTER.

Ronnie Sox:
"Your fuel system has to be dead right."

"I don't care how much horsepower you've got. If you don't feed it, it's not going to live. It's not going to work. Your fuel system has to be dead right."

That's Ronnie Sox of the winning Sox and Martin team talking. Fresh from sweeping the 1967 Spring Nationals Super Stock Eliminator, low ET, top MPH and SS/B class, Ronnie had some things to say about the

Inside The Boss:
"If Carters work on the track, they're going to work on the street or anywhere."

fuel system in "The Boss," his '67 Plymouth GTX.

He uses Carter. Every time out. "In drag racing you need instant go. You've got to have it as soon as you punch it. The acceleration on the Carter carbs is real positive. Once we get the jetting right, all we ever change is the heat range of the plugs when the temperature changes. I'm always sure I'm going to get the best out of the engine every time.

"We drive a legal car, so we can't

bore the interior or anything like that. If Carters work on the track, they're going to work on the street or anywhere. We like them. They do a good job for us."

If you drive for bucks, cups or just good performance, better check out Carter carbs, fuel pumps and filters. The Carter electric pump feeds 72 gph, the highest of any in-line unit available anywhere.

CARTER EQUIPPED

Get two Carter Decals. Just send 25¢ to: "Carter Decals," P. O. Box 6373, Fairgrounds Station, St. Louis, Mo. 63107

acf

Carter Carburetor Division

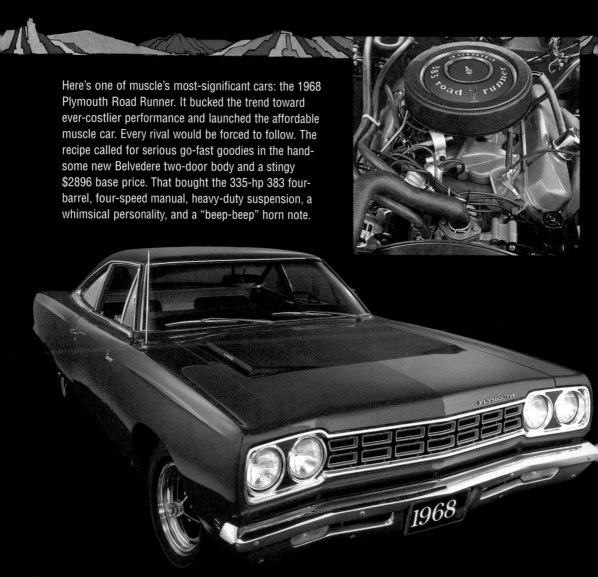

Here's one of muscle's most-significant cars: the 1968 Plymouth Road Runner. It bucked the trend toward ever-costlier performance and launched the affordable muscle car. Every rival would be forced to follow. The recipe called for serious go-fast goodies in the handsome new Belvedere two-door body and a stingy $2896 base price. That bought the 335-hp 383 four-barrel, four-speed manual, heavy-duty suspension, a whimsical personality, and a "beep-beep" horn note.

"Beep-Beep!"

HeMi

A 383 Road Runner turned 15-second ETs. Low 13s were $714 away via the sole engine option: the 426 Hemi. Plymouth forecast sales of just 2500 Road Runners for '68; the final tally was 45,000, 1019 of which had Hemis. It paid Warner Bros. $50,000 for the cartoon bird's likeness, while the division's own promotional art was part of the brilliant marketing. The car attracted hard-core drivers and casual enthusiasts alike.

GTX continued atop Plymouth's midsize line for '68. Like Road Runner, it was based on the mainstream Belvedere/Satellite, but came standard with stuff Road Runner didn't even offer, such as buckets and the 440-cid Super Commando V-8. They shared the Hemi option, but only GTX offered a convertible body style. It started at $3590, $235 more than the hardtop, and accounted for 1026 of 19,940 GTXs sold for '68. Just 450 in total had a Hemi. A four-speed with pistol-grip shifter was a no-cost option.

1968

Barracuda started carving a legit muscle profile in 1967 when it got a larger new body and an available 280-hp 383. The '68s celebrated on these pages could have a tough little 340 V-8 underrated at 275 hp, or a 383 bumped to 300 hp. A select few pro drag racers were able to land competition-only Hemi Barracudas built for Plymouth by Hurst Performance. They turned high 9s. Plymouth's pop-art promotions were late-'60s treasures.

Road Runner's looks were little-altered for '69, but its budget-bomb feel was, with new options like power windows, bucket seats, and a convertible body style. The 335-hp 383 was again standard, a Hemi the top option, and a 390-hp triple-two-barrel-carb 440 a midyear addition. Sox & Martin's Hemi Road Runner ran 10.94 at 128.3 to capture the AHRA Top Stock Eliminator crown.

The hood vents on the Road Runner (this page) and the GTX (opposite) were decorative unless you ordered the optional "Air Grabber" setup, which was standard with the Hemi. It fed cool air via an under-hood collar that closed around the air cleaner. Plymouth's promotional illustrations were the period's most evocative, conveying in caricature the power and personality of its muscle cars. By '69, the artwork's tone had evolved from love-in bright to a darker, acid-trip style so wonderfully represented here.

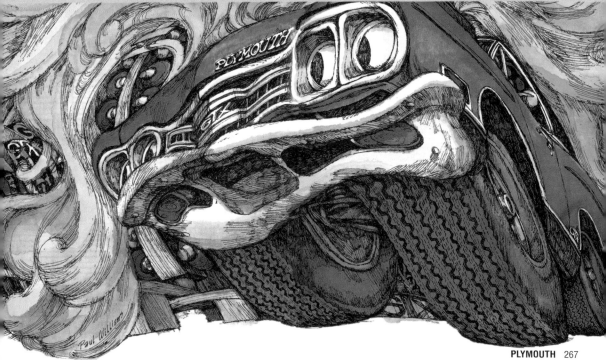

Paul William?

Plymouth coined the 'Cuda name to identify enthusiast versions of its '69 Barracuda fastbacks and coupes with 340- or 383-cid V-8s. The baddest '69 street 'Cuda arrived midyear with a 375-hp 440, mandatory TorqueFlite, and fake hood scoops. It did 0-60 in 5.6 seconds, the quarter in 14.0 at 104 mph. Lighting up pro drag ranks were wheel-lifting, slick-wrinkling 9-second Hemi versions, led by the always clean, fast Sox & Martin.

270

Opposite ends of the 1970 Plymouth performance spectrum: the Sport Fury GT (left) and the new compact Duster 340 (above). The former listed for $3898 and was a full-size hardtop outfitted with the 440 V-8, high-upshift TorqueFlite, and heavy-duty everything. Duster was basically a Valiant economy car with a fastback body. In 340 form, it got the scrappy 275-hp four-barrel—which actually had about 325 hp—and ran 14.7 quarters. At a base price of just $2547, it was another Plymouth budget-muscle home run with 24,817 sales for the year. This one's color was called Moulin Rouge.

Redesigned to share platform and powertrains with the new Dodge Challenger, the '70 Barracuda was a muscle milestone. 'Cuda performance included the Trans Am-inspired AAR with three two-barrel carbs and Hemi models, which were at home in the NHRA's new Pro Stock class. Right: This Hemi Cuda promo was a high-water mark in muscle-era artwork.

Plymouth coined "The Rapid Transit System" to market its '70 performance cars. Members were the 'Cudas and Duster 340, Sport Fury GT, and, on display here in a boss factory shot, the reskinned GTX and Road Runner. Engines carried over and included the "440+6" triple-two-barrel 440. Standard with a Hemi, optional with a 440, the functional new Air Grabber hood duct rose menacingly via an under-dash switch. On Plymouth's color palette were hues named Lemon Twist, Tor-Red, Vitamin C, Lime Light, and In Violet Metallic, among others.

Plymouth's companion to the wild '69 Dodge Daytona was the Road Runner-based 1970 Superbird. These were offered to the public to qualify race versions for NASCAR. The metal nosecone (with headlamps in flip-up fiberglass tubs) and aluminum tail wing were aero aids at Superspeedway speeds, but added 400 pounds to road models. Street editions had the 440 four-barrel or the Hemi. The aero add-ons were of less value at the drag strip, but Sox & Martin ran a mean 'Bird in the NHRA's Modified Production division.

'cuda

Barracuda sacrificed some of its clean looks for '71 to a busy quad-lamp grille, decorative fender gills, and tarted-up tail. But while rivals dialed back on performance to appease emissions and insurance concerns, Dodge and Plymouth still offered a broad muscle range. 'Cudas again featured 340, 383, 440, and 426 Hemi power. Also back was the shaker scoop. Standard on Hemis, optional with other 'Cuda mills, this functional piece mounted to the air cleaner and shook through a hole in the hood as the engine rocked.

As if taunting the growing anti-muscle car forces, Plymouth performance was bolder-looking than ever in '71. Exhibit A was a 'Cuda with optional "billboard" bodyside graphics. This one also sports the standard 'Cuda hood with nonfunctional scoops. Still, Barracuda sales fell 66 percent. Right: Interest remained high in pro drags. Here, driver Ronnie Sox guides his 'Cuda to the starting line.

383

Buddy Martin handled the business end and Ronnie Sox worked magic with a four-speed manual to make a legendary Pro Stock team. Their '71 Duster rode a Hemi to 9-second ETs. Top engine in customer Dusters was again the 275-hp 340. It was no sleeper slathered in "Sassy Grass Green" and outfitted with the optional flat-black hood/340-script treatment. Groovy. Duster sales were up 21 percent for the year, but sales of the 340 fell by half. Muscle was in trouble.

GTX and Road Runner were radically reshaped for '71. Wheelbase was shorter and rear track wider for better handling. Interiors were new, and the convertible was retired. This would be GTX's final model year and it went out with the 440 four-barrel, now at 370 hp, the triple-deuce 440 at 385, or the Hemi, at 425. Road Runner (right) returned with its 383 detuned to 300 hp but big-block options—and a sense of humor—were still afoot.

440·6

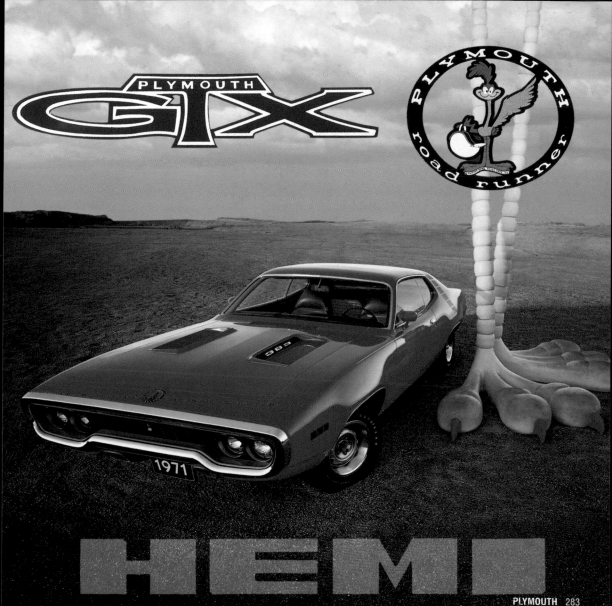

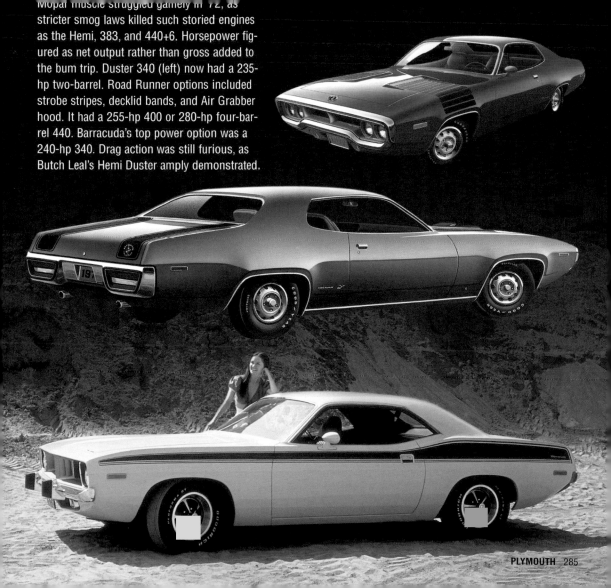

Mopar muscle struggled gamely in '72, as stricter smog laws killed such storied engines as the Hemi, 383, and 440+6. Horsepower figured as net output rather than gross added to the bum trip. Duster 340 (left) now had a 235-hp two-barrel. Road Runner options included strobe stripes, decklid bands, and Air Grabber hood. It had a 255-hp 400 or 280-hp four-barrel 440. Barracuda's top power option was a 240-hp 340. Drag action was still furious, as Butch Leal's Hemi Duster amply demonstrated.

A 363-hp Super Duty 389 was the top Pontiac engine at the beginning of 1961. Late in the model year, Pontiac unleashed the Super Duty 421, rated at 405 horsepower with dual quads. Unique 8-lug wheels were a $107 option. The wheel rim bolted to the outer portion of the aluminum brake drum, which doubled as the wheel hub and was finned to improve brake cooling. Ace Wilson's Royal Pontiac dealership in Royal Oak, Michigan, emerged as the quasi-official performance arm of the factory. A Royal-prepped, Hurst-equipped Catalina served as a top prize at the '61 NHRA Nationals.

moving machine either side of the line!

Pontiac Catalina

There's a good deal more to driving than a straight-line quarter-mile, and nobody knows that better than the performance-minded. Which is why Pontiac's Catalina shows up so often among you people.

One of the reasons for this popularity is the choice of engine/transmission teams. Standard equipment is a 215-hp Trophy V-8 hooked up to a three-speed stick, of course. But you can get a storming 405-horse engine and heavy-duty four-speed as extra-cost options. And other extra-cost options blanket the area in between, including automatics.

Wide-Track and Pontiac's own special handling precision come standard with the Catalina, naturally. So does

a fat helping of pure luxury, without which you shouldn't allow yourself to be.

The great thing is that a new Catalina goes easy on your bankroll—this is Pontiac's lowest-priced full-sized series. Talk it over with your Pontiac dealer first chance you get. Plan to spend some time with him—you could use up a whole day just looking through that list of options, and a happier time you couldn't imagine.

(Oh, and if you'd like to check your Cat against the clocks, feel free. No fair making the Catalina do the pushing while the dragster has all the fun.) Pontiac Motor Division, General Motors Corporation.

Pontiac's "personal luxury" Grand Prix (above) debuted in mid-'62 with standard bucket seats and 389 power. Super Duty 421 Catalinas continued to assault the drag strips. Absence of chrome scripts on the front fenders helps identify the Catalina below as one of the aluminum body-panel-equipped cars. Price of its dual-quad 421 engine alone was $2250, but included three-inch exhaust cutouts that could be unbolted to free up more power. The 421's available aluminum exhaust manifolds were for drag racing only; they would melt if subjected to the sustained heat of normal driving. Note the tow-bar mounts under the bumper of Royal's Catalina two-door sedan.

BITES LIKE THIS

LOOKS LIKE THIS

RACEMASTER DRAGSTER

SEND TODAY FOR FREE CATALOG. ENCLOSE 10¢ FOR DECAL. M & H TIRE CO., 433 MAIN ST., WATERTOWN 72, MASS.

Pontiac built six 1963 Tempest wagons with Super Duty 421s for A/FX competition. Wagon bodies were used with the goal of getting more weight over the rear wheels for extra traction; ETs were in the high 11s. Stacked headlamps and fresh sheetmetal identified full-size '63 Pontiacs. *Motor Trend* ran a four-speed dual-quad Super Duty Catalina to a 0-60 run of 5.4 seconds and a quarter mile of 13.9 at 107—on street tires.

The 1964 Tempest GTO is generally credited with kick-starting the muscle car era. There were hot production vehicles before it, but the GTO was the first midsize car to be conceived and marketed as a total performance package that was aimed at enthusiast drivers. Base engine was a 325-hp four-barrel 389. A 348-hp Tri-Power version was optional.

GTOs got vertical headlights and other styling updates for 1965. While other manufacturers were still hustling to get true muscle cars to market, the GTO had already become a bona-fide pop-culture phenomenon. Hurst awarded a brand-new customized GTO (right) to the contestant who correctly counted the number of times the word "tiger" was heard in the song "GeeTO Tiger." (The correct answer was 42.) The Tri-Power 389 gained 12 hp, to 360.

Count the tigers!

Listen to the Colpix recording "GeeTO Tiger" by the Tigers (a great new group of swingers), and count the number of times the word tiger is sung in the record. (Complete rules are listed below.)

And win one in the HURST-GeeTO Tiger Contest!

Sound the trumpets or something, Hurst is out with the safest custom wheel ever made! The only forged wheel in the industry!

HURST

GTO

CALIFORNIA
1ONR GTO
PONTIAC GTO

The GTO was still Tempest-based, but became a series all its own for 1966. Redesigned bodies had a handsome "Coke bottle" shape. The four-barrel 389 continued at 335 hp. The $113 triple-two-barrel had 360 with or without Ram Air, but production ceased at midyear when GM outlawed multi-carb engines for all but the Corvette. GTOs were relentlessly promoted as drag racing machines; here, two "GeeTO Tigers" vie for C/Stock honors at the NHRA Nationals.

These were fat times for Pontiac. GTO output hit 81,722 in 1967, after a record high of 96,946 for 1966. The '67 Goats got minor styling updates such as a mesh grille and a resculpted tail, and a 400-cid V-8 replaced the 389. A $263 Ram Air package included hardware that opened the otherwise nonfunctional hood scoops, plus a pan that went around the open-element air cleaner and mated to the hood with a foam rubber skirt. Royal Pontiac offered a "Royal Bobcat" tune-up package that included thinner head gaskets for higher compression, rejetted carb, and decals to let the in-crowd know that this was no ordinary GTO.

There's only one Great One.

We've been proving it for five years.

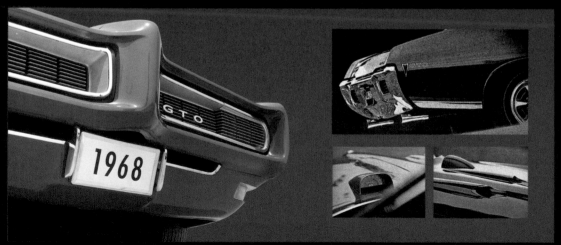

1968

GTOs got a dazzling new shape with an ener-
gy-absorbing Endura front bumper for 1968.
Hidden headlamps were so popular that
most people didn't realize they were an
option, as were dual exhaust splitters, a
hood-mounted tach, and functional Ram Air
scoops. Top GTO engine choice was the
366-hp Ram Air II 400. The 1968 Firebirds
were nearly identical to the inaugural '67s
save for side marker lamps and the deletion
of vent windows. The 400 V-8 (right) added
five horses to both base and Ram Air versions (now 330 and 335 hp).

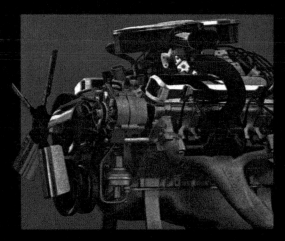

The 1969 Firebirds wore new sheetmetal as well as revised front and rear styling. In March 1969, Pontiac unleashed the $725 Trans Am Performance and Appearance package with little fanfare. To the Firebird it added a functional twin-scoop hood, rear spoiler, open fender vents, and a unique white and blue paint scheme. Just 697 coupes and eight convertibles were built. Top engine option for both Firebird 400 HOs and Trans Ams was the 345-hp Ram Air IV 400. A four-speed and 3.90:1 cogs came with the Ram Air IV, though a three-speed automatic was optional. A hood-mounted tach was an $85 option.

"The Great One" got minor styling updates and a whimsical new performance model for 1969. Pontiac added op-art decals, a rear spoiler, and a 366-hp Ram Air III 400 to create The Judge, a $332 option package on the GTO. The car's name was a sly pop-culture reference—"Here come da Judge" was a recurring catchphrase on the TV show *Laugh-In*. The first 5000 Judges were painted Carousel Red (a bright shade of orange), but other colors were offered. The 370-hp Ram Air IV was a $390 Judge option.

With the introduction of the second-generation Firebird in 1970, Pontiac's Trans Am came into its own as a bare-knuckles brawler. Functional spoilers and vents abounded, while super-tough underpinnings and quickened steering gave it corner-hungry handling. Only the strongest 400-cid V-8s were offered; a 345-hp Ram Air 400 was standard, while a 375-hp Ram Air IV was optional. The Firebird Formula 400 shed the Trans Am's spoilers and swapped out the "shaker" hood for a twin-scooped fiberglass unit. The scoops were functional when Ram Air was ordered. All Firebirds got a body-color Endura front bumper.

The reskinned 1970 GTOs wore a new Endura nose with exposed headlamps. The Judge was a $337 option, which again included wild graphics, a wing, and a standard 366-hp Ram Air III mill. Eye-popping Orbit Orange paint was exclusive to the Judge. The LeMans GT-37 was introduced as "poor man's GTO." Available in a two-door sedan body style, the GT-37 came standard with a 255-hp 350 and a three-speed, but could be equipped with a four-barrel 400 and a four-speed.

Insurance rates and changing tastes retired the Judge in mid-1971 after just 374 had been built. Likewise, the budget-minded GT-37 LeMans was dropped after a minuscule production run. The Trans Am was taking over as Pontiac's premier performance car. The T/A was unchanged externally, but packed a strong new 335-hp 455 HO underhood. Royal Pontiac had been at it for nearly a decade by '71, and its Firebird Formulas were just as formidable in Super Stock competition as they were on the street.

GTO

455 CID

For '72, the GTO was demoted to option status and looked all but identical to the '71 models. The '72 Firebirds were visually unchanged save for a honeycomb mesh grille insert. Both GTOs and Firebird Formulas could get a four-barrel 455 HO that was good for 300 net hp. *Motor Trend*'s 455 HO Goat turned a 15.4 ET at 92 mph. Pontiac's optional "honeycomb" wheels offered a distinctive appearance, but were especially heavy due to their polyurethane/steel construction.